★ World War II ★

THE WAR AT HOME

by Stuart A. Kallen

Titles in The American War Library series include:

World War II
Hitler and the Nazis
Kamikazes
Leaders and Generals
Life as a POW
Life of an American Soldier in Europe
Strategic Battles in Europe
Strategic Battles in the Pacific
The War at Home
Weapons of War

The Civil War
Leaders of the North and South
Life Among the Soldiers and Cavalry
Lincoln and the Abolition of Slavery
Strategic Battles
Weapons of War

World War II

THE WAR AT HOME

by Stuart A. Kallen

Lucent Books, P.O. Box 289011, San Diego, CA 92198-9011

Library of Congress Cataloging-in-Publication Data

Kallen, Stuart A., 1955–
    The war at home / by Stuart A. Kallen.
        p.   cm.—(The American war library series)
    Includes bibliographical references (p.   ) and index.
    Summary: Discusses the impact of World War II on life in the
United States, including preparations for the war, civil defense,
the changing work force, family life, and the end of the war.
    ISBN 1-56006-531-1 (lib. bdg. : alk. paper)
    1. World War, 1939–1945—Juvenile literature. [1. World War,
1939–1945—United States.] I. Title. II. Series.
D743.7.K26   2000
940.53—dc21   99-29210
                                                                        CIP

Copyright 2000 by Lucent Books, Inc.
P.O. Box 289011, San Diego, California 92198-9011

Printed in the U.S.A.

★ Contents ★

A Nation Forged by War

The United States, like many nations, was forged and defined by war. Despite Benjamin Franklin's opinion that "There never was a good war or a bad peace," the United States owes its very existence to the War of Independence, one to which Franklin wholeheartedly subscribed. The country forged by war in 1776 was tempered and made stronger by the Civil War in the 1860s.

The Texas Revolution, the Mexican-American War, and the Spanish-American War expanded the country's borders and gave it overseas possessions. These wars made the United States a world power, but this status came with a price, as the nation became a key but reluctant player in both World War I and World War II.

Each successive war further defined the country's role on the world stage. Following World War II, U.S. foreign policy redefined itself to focus on the role of defender, not only of the freedom of its own citizens, but also of the freedom of people everywhere. During the cold war that followed World War II until the collapse of the Soviet Union, defending the world meant fighting communism. This goal, manifested in the Korean and Vietnam conflicts, proved elusive, and soured the American public on its achievability. As the United States emerged as the world's sole superpower, American foreign policy has been guided less by national interest and more on protecting international human rights. But as involvement in Somalia and Kosovo prove, this goal has been equally elusive.

As a result, the country's view of itself changed. Bolstered by victories in World Wars I and II, Americans first relished the role of protector. But, as war followed war in a seemingly endless procession, Americans began to doubt their leaders, their motives, and themselves. The Vietnam War especially caused people to question the validity of sending its young people to die in places where they were not particularly wanted and for people who did not seem especially grateful.

While the most obvious changes brought about by America's wars have been geopolitical in nature, many other aspects of society have been touched. War often does not bring about change directly, but acts instead like the catalyst in a chemical reaction, accelerating changes already in progress.

Some of these changes have been societal. The role of women in the United States had been slowly changing, but World War II put thousands into the workforce and into uniform. They might have gone back to being housewives after the war, but equality, once experienced, would not be forgotten.

Likewise, wars have accelerated technological change. The necessity for faster airplanes and a more destructive bomb led to the development of jet planes and nuclear energy. Artificial fibers developed for parachutes in the 1940s were used in the clothing of the 1950s.

Lucent Books' American War Library covers key wars in the development of the nation. Each war is covered in several volumes, to allow for more detail, context, and to provide volumes on often neglected subjects, such as the kamikazes of World War II, or weapons used in the Civil War. As with all Lucent Books, notes, annotated bibliographies, and appendixes such as glossaries give students a launching point for further research. In addition, sidebars and archival photographs enhance the text. Together, each volume in The American War Library will aid students in understanding how America's wars have shaped and changed its politics, economics, and society.

Before the War

For most Americans World War II clearly began at 7:50 A.M. on the fateful Sunday morning of December 7, 1941, when a cloud of Japanese warplanes darkened the skies over the American naval base at Pearl Harbor on the island of Oahu, Hawaii. Forty-three Mitsubishi fighter planes and 140 Nakajima bombers swooped down, bombing, torpedoing, and strafing the U.S. Pacific Fleet. An hour later a second wave of 183 Japanese fighters and bombers struck. Twenty-one U.S. ships were hit, and more than 200 aircraft were destroyed or damaged. In addition, the attack destroyed about 75 percent of the aircraft on airfields around Pearl Harbor.

The battleship *Arizona* was destroyed, the *West Virginia* and *California* were sunk (but later raised and repaired), and the *Nevada* was heavily damaged.

Approximately 2,403 people, mostly American service personnel, were killed. More than 1,100 people were wounded, and 1,000 more were missing. Japanese losses were fewer than 100 casualties, 29 planes, and 5 midget submarines. For security reasons, the details of America's loss at Pearl Harbor were not released for one year.

The Japanese attack on Pearl Harbor on December 7, 1941, galvanized American support for involvement in World War II.

Within twenty-four hours of the attack, President Franklin Roosevelt signed Joint Senate Resolution 116, which declared, "A state of war exists between the Imperial Government of Japan and the Government and People of the United States." Roosevelt later addressed a joint session of Congress with these words:

> Yesterday, Dec. 7, 1941—a date which will live in infamy—the United States of America was suddenly and deliberately attacked by naval and air forces of the empire of Japan. . . . I ask that the Congress declare that since the unprovoked and dastardly attack by Japan on Sunday . . . a state of war has existed be-

Franklin Delano Roosevelt signs the declaration of war against Japan in December 1941 after the bombing of Pearl Harbor.

tween the United States and the Japanese Empire.[1]

The attack on Pearl Harbor had been personally approved by Tojo Hideki, Japan's prime minister and a leading advocate of Japanese military conquest. Tojo believed that the Japanese had scored a brilliant tactical victory at Pearl Harbor by crippling U.S. naval power in the Pacific.

But the attack proved to be a psychological blunder on the part of the Japanese leadership: Prior to Pearl Harbor most Americans had wanted to stay out of the wars fought by the Japanese in China and elsewhere. After the attack American public opinion was mobilized against Japan.

In a tactical error, the Japanese failed to blow up the Pacific Fleet's fuel supply along with three aircraft carriers that were at sea at the time. This allowed an immediate U.S. offensive that would have been delayed for months if the fuel had been destroyed.

The Dirty Thirties

World War II began for America that day, but in reality the events of the 1930s were more responsible for World War II than the Japanese attack. The 1930s were marked by the Great Depression, which was unique in its magnitude of economic torment. During the darkest days of 1933, one out of four Americans was out of work, and the huge economic slump continued throughout the thirties, shaking the foundations of American capitalism.

The stark numbers illustrate the distress of millions who lost jobs, savings, farms, and homes. From 1930 to 1933 industrial stocks lost 80 percent of their value. In the four years from 1929 to 1932, approximately eleven thousand U.S. banks failed (44 percent of the total), and about $2 billion in deposits evaporated. The gross national product, which had been growing for years at an average annual rate of 3.5 percent, declined at a rate of over 10 percent annually. Agricultural distress was intense: Farm prices fell by 53 percent from 1929 to 1932.

When Roosevelt was elected president in 1932, he instituted a series of government programs to help financially strapped Americans. The Civilian Conservation Corps took young men off the streets and sent them out to plant forests, clear trails, build picnic shelters, and per-

Their efforts at finding work thwarted by the Great Depression, these men sit idly on a park bench. Three out of four Americans were out of work.

form other outdoor work in recreation areas. The government refinanced about 20 percent of farm mortgages through the Farm Credit Administration. The Works Progress Administration employed over 2 million people in jobs ranging from laborers to musicians and writers. The Public Works Administration spent about $4 billion on the construction of highways and public buildings in the years 1933–1939. But in spite of the government's best intentions, unemployment was still at 17.2 percent at the end of the 1930s.

Although Americans suffered, many Europeans were even harder hit by the economic crisis. They had never recovered from World War I (1914–1918), which left much of Europe in ruins. When the Great Depression caused world trade to fall off, many countries turned inward and became loudly nationalistic—strongly devoted to the interests of their own culture and nation.

At the same time, Germany was suffering under the sanctions imposed by the victors of World War I. The country was forced to admit responsibility for the war, give up territory, disarm, and pay millions of dollars in reparations to the nations that had been damaged by German invasion.

The payment of reparations placed an enormous strain on a country already bankrupted by war. As inflation mounted, German money became worthless. Adolf Hitler and the Nazi Party took over the government in 1932 promising to enact radical solutions to economic problems and to defend nationalistic values.

Japan had been on the winning side in World War I, but many Japanese people were also dissatisfied with their country's status, believing that Japan should be the dominant power in Asia. Military officers in particular held this view. Although Japan had a pro-Western government during the 1920s, the military remained a guiding force in political affairs.

The aftermath of World War I and the hardships caused by the Great Depression

A German woman lights the fire in her stove using worthless paper money. The payment of war reparations decimated Germany's economic system.

contributed to the tensions that produced World War II. Ironically, the massive military buildup caused by World War II provided the economic stimulus that finally ended the depression.

Local Battles Lead to World War

Like lightning strikes turning several small fires into a massive conflagration, World War II began in dozens of small battles around the world. In 1931 Japanese troops invaded and quickly conquered the Chinese province of Manchuria after claiming that Chinese saboteurs were tampering with a Japanese-owned railway there. The League of Nations, formed after World War I to oppose such aggression, condemned the Japanese, who quit the league and kept Manchuria.

Meanwhile, many Germans felt that American-style democracy had failed their country after World War I. They looked with increasing favor on antidemocratic fascist elements that glorified war as the means of national salvation. By taking advantage of this sentiment, Adolf Hitler—a member of the Nazi (National Socialist) Party—was elected chancellor in 1933.

Hitler took Germany out of the League of Nations and began a massive program to build up the defenses of the German army, navy, and air force. In March 1935 he restored universal military service.

Italy also embraced Fascism when dictator Benito Mussolini came to power in 1922. Mussolini, seeking an easy foreign victory to galvanize his country, invaded the African nation of Ethiopia in 1935. The highly trained and modernized Italian army easily conquered the untrained and poorly armed Ethiopians.

In 1936 the Spanish civil war broke out between leftist coalitions and fascist rightists led by General Francisco Franco. The war soon drew international attention as Hitler and Mussolini sent planes, troops, and supplies to Franco. This cooperation cemented relations between the Axis powers of Germany and Italy. To counter the threat, the Soviet Union (USSR) supplied military equipment to Spanish leftists.

Pre–World War II firestorms reached a climax when Hitler's Nazis conquered Austria and Czechoslovakia in 1938. In the spring of 1939 France and Great Britain guaranteed Poland's safety against German aggression. In September 1939, however, Hitler's military machine struck at Poland.

In what was known as a blitzkrieg (lightning war), high-speed panzer (tank) units pushed across the borders, blasting holes in

Benito Mussolini and Adolf Hitler sent military supplies in support of Francisco Franco during the Spanish civil war in 1936.

Polish defenses. From the skies Luftwaffe (air force) bombers destroyed the Polish air force. The Nazi attack on Poland prompted Great Britain and France to declare war on Germany.

In August 1940 the Nazis' Luftwaffe began an all-out air war—known as the blitz—on British ports, airfields, industrial centers, and, finally, on London. In 1941 Hitler's blitzkrieg quickly conquered France.

The United States Prepares to Fight

Most Americans—remembering the horrors of World War I—wanted to remain far removed from Europe's problems. Nonetheless, Roosevelt and Congress began to prepare for what seemed inevitable. In September 1940 the first-ever peacetime draft law went into effect in the United States, requiring the registration of 17 million men. In March 1941 Congress passed the Lend-Lease Act, empowering the president to allow shipment of vital war materials to Great Britain. Later that year the Lend-Lease Act was extended to include China (under attack from Japan) and the USSR (threatened by Germany).

Americans also took measures to defend the Western Hemisphere by stationing forces in both Greenland and Iceland to patrol the Atlantic Ocean. Likewise, after the sinking of U.S.–owned ships in August and September 1941, U.S. merchant vessels were authorized to arm themselves.

A newsboy holds out papers announcing Japan's Pearl Harbor attack, which drew the United States into the war.

Following the Pearl Harbor attack, the United States declared war on Japan on December 8, 1941. On December 11 Germany and Italy declared war on the United States. The European and Japanese wars now merged into one world conflict. And in the United States, people pulled together in a stunning show of unity that would help end the fascist aggression by 1945.

Chapter 1

Preparing for War

The surprise attack on Pearl Harbor caused widespread panic on America's west coast. Cities from Seattle to San Diego were gripped with what the navy's official history later described as "plain, simple, mass hysteria." As the Associated Press wrote,

> No [comfort] was offered by Lt. Gen. John DeWitt, head of the Western Defense Command, who told San Franciscans that "death and destruction are likely to come to this city at any moment" and claimed that enemy planes had flown over the city. "Why bombs were not dropped," he said, "I do not know." [2]

Three days after the Pearl Harbor assault, the army declared the west coast, a theater of operations, or a war zone. Rumors of war were rampant. People claimed that Japanese-American farmers had planted crops to form arrows that pointed toward military bases. Brigadier General William Ord Ryan claimed that a large number of unidentified planes flew over the Golden Gate Bridge one night but turned back for reasons unknown. (They later turned out to be U.S. Army Air Force planes.)

American Cities Prepare for War

People up and down the west coast of America were ordered to turn out all their lights or tack thick black curtains up over their windows so that bombers could not see house lights in the event of an air raid. Gun emplacements sprouted overnight on the rooftops of major cities and coastal towns, and searchlights swayed across the skies searching for enemy planes. Citizens began to dig bomb shelters and to inspect caves and mining shafts as places of refuge. In Washington, D.C., gunnery crews maintained vigils next to the Washington Monument and other federal buildings, and the White House windows were blacked out.

On the day after the attack on Pearl Harbor, sixty army trucks in San Francisco rushed antiaircraft guns to the water's edge near the Golden Gate Bridge. Air-raid sirens screamed nonstop as air wardens rushed from house to house darkening lights. Numerous automobiles crashed into each other in the darkness. Nerves were so frayed that a sentry shot and seriously wounded a female motorist on the Bay Bridge who was slow to halt at a checkpoint.

Women put up quilted fabric to blacken out their windows in case of a Japanese air attack on the United States.

In Los Angeles, a service bulletin ordered a blackout of all lights within a fifteen-mile radius of the harbor, and all radio stations were ordered off the air at 7:00 P.M. (Enemy aircraft could tune in to radio signals to direct their planes to land.)

Irrational behavior marked the confusion that came on the heels of Pearl Harbor. In Los Angeles, a jittery antiaircraft battery blazed away in panic at imaginary warplanes. The shell fragments fell on the city and injured dozens of residents. In Seattle, during one of the frequent false air-raid alerts, a mob of 1,000 angry citizens smashed the windows and looted stores that did not turn out their lights. In New York City, a false air-raid alarm caused school officials to release over 1 million schoolchildren from their classrooms. In the confusion, hundreds of students were directed to air-raid shelters while distraught parents searched the streets for their children.

Air-Raid Instructions

The Office of Civilian Defense issued a series of instructions for Americans to heed during air raids on the west coast. They were reprinted in the book *World War II, 1939–1945.*

> The safest place in an air raid is at home. If you are away from home, get under cover of the nearest shelter. Avoid crowded places. Stay out of the streets.
>
> The enemy wants you to run out into the streets, create a mob, start a panic. Don't do it!
>
> If incendiary bombs fall, [shoot a light] spray from a garden hose (never a splash or stream) of water on the bomb. Switch to a stream to put out any fire started by the bomb. Switch back to a spray for the bomb.
>
> The bomb will burn for about 15 minutes if left alone, only about two minutes under a fine water spray. A jet splash, stream, or bucket of water will make it explode.
>
> If you have a soda-and-acid extinguisher (the kind you turn upside down), use it with your finger over the nozzle to make a spray. Don't use the chemical kind (small cylinders of liquid) on bombs. It is all right for ordinary fires.
>
> Should gas be used, go at once to the most "inside room" in your house (fewest doors and windows). Paste paper over glass. Stuff rags in window cracks and under doors.

> But above all, keep cool, stay home. Choose one member of the family to be the home air-raid warden who will remember the rules and what to do.

As part of a training exercise to combat the effects of chemical warfare during a possible air raid, a Red Cross driver learns to use a gas mask.

Meanwhile, in British Columbia, Canada, a nightly blackout of all coastal areas on the Pacific coast was ordered because, according to reports, "an attack by Japanese forces of the Pacific northwest coast is imminent."[3] All motor traffic was halted at 6:00 P.M., and the drivers were ordered home by naval policemen.

While west coast fears may have been justified in the weeks following Pearl Harbor, Americans felt threatened in nearly every village and city in the nation. In Georgia, a citizens' army of men too old, young, or sick to serve in the military set about preparing embankments along the Atlantic coast for a possible German invasion. In Arizona, residents prepared for an attack that might come through Mexico. In Wisconsin, the head of the American Legion proposed a guerrilla army to be formed from the state's twenty-five thousand licensed deer hunters—"a formidable foe for any attackers,"[4] he insisted.

As Christmas passed and 1942 began without an enemy attack, Americans turned their attentions to the more serious work of raising an army and sending soldiers to fight in far-off foreign lands across both the Pacific and Atlantic Oceans.

America Joins Up

The Pearl Harbor attack united Americans as never before. In the wake of the attack almost everyone, it seemed, wanted to enlist in the war effort. Army and navy recruiting stations were deluged with volunteers. They included farm kids, baseball heroes, doctors, blue-collar workers, and even Hollywood film stars.

Three generations of one Detroit family—grandfather, father, and son—showed up at a local recruiting station. In Washington, D.C., eighty-one-year-old John Pershing, general of the army during World War I, checked out of the hospital and was driven to the White House to volunteer his services. In Hollywood, most of the leading men were soon in uniform—film star Jimmy Stewart fattened up his skinny frame to make the air force's minimum weight requirement. In New York, baseball hero

Many famous people joined the war effort, including ballplayer Joe DiMaggio. DiMaggio traded a fifty-six consecutive game hitting streak for an enlistment in the army air force.

"Joltin'" Joe DiMaggio put down his mitt and picked up a gun for Uncle Sam. (DiMaggio was on a fifty-six-consecutive-game hitting streak when he joined up.) Anyone who was of military age and was not wearing a uniform was either physically or mentally impaired or was openly questioned about his patriotism.

War and Baseball

At the outbreak of World War II, amateur and professional sporting events were widely popular in the United States. Although sports never stopped during the war, the draft considerably affected many sports teams. Baseball was the most popular American sport at the time—and the hardest hit.

More than fifty-seven hundred men played in the major and minor leagues in 1941, and more than four thousand of them eventually served in the military. The number of minor-league teams shrank from forty-one at the start of the war to nine during the war. To save power, night baseball was suspended until 1944, resulting in many twilight games.

President Roosevelt, however, advocated the continuation of baseball. In a letter to the baseball commissioner in 1942, according to *V for Victory* by Stan B. Cohen, the president stated:

Baseball provides a recreation which does not last over two hours . . . and which can be got for very little cost. . . . Three-hundred teams use 5,000 or 6,000 players, these players are a definite recreational asset to at least 20,000,000 of their fellow citizens—and that in my judgment is thoroughly worthwhile.

During the two and a half years of the war, major-league teams used players who were very young or called older men out of retirement. Travel restrictions were imposed, and the government limited spring training.

In all, over one thousand professional ball players from the American and National Leagues served in the military between 1942 and 1945.

The Selective Service

Although many men volunteered to join the military, a full two-thirds were drafted. Until 1940, the United States had been one of the world's few countries where military service was not mandatory. But in September of that year, Congress approved the Selective Training and Service Act—the first peacetime draft in American history. This highly controversial bill was only approved after weeks of highly charged debate.

The Selective Service law required all men between the ages of twenty-one and thirty-five to register with their local draft boards on October 16. On that day the country's 6,175 draft boards signed up 16.3 million men. The men included truck drivers and executives, ranchers and Rockefellers. Special draft boards were set up inside state and federal prisons and more than one hundred thousand nonviolent felons were taken into the armed forces. These men were convicted of felonies such as drug use and embezzlement.

Every man who registered received a draft number. Two weeks after registration, Roosevelt met with Secretary of War Henry Stimson to pull numbered slips of paper from a giant glass bowl. The numbers would determine who would be drafted. The numbers were in bright blue capsules and went from number one to nine thousand, corresponding with numbers handed out at local draft boards.

When the moment came, millions of Americans tuned in on their radios. Secretary Stimson was blindfolded with a swatch of upholstery taken from a chair used 164 years earlier by the signers of the Declaration of Independence. After Stimson picked a number, he handed it to Roosevelt, who read the number into his radio microphone. The number was

158. Across the land there were 6,175 men who held that number. In this manner millions of men were drafted.

Once the numbers were chosen, questionnaires concerning the draftee's health and vital statistics were sent out by local draft boards to everyone whose number was picked. The draft boards—made up of local citizens—assigned numbers to each draftee. There were more than a dozen classifications that ranged from 1-A (available for military service) to 4-F (physically, mentally, or morally unfit for service).

Franklin Delano Roosevelt (left) looks on as secretary of war Henry L. Stimson draws the first draft numbers on October 29, 1940.

Those who were 1-A quickly received a form letter explaining that the draft board had determined that the reader was to be "notified that you have been selected for training and service in the Army."[5]

Men who did not volunteer were drafted into the army. Others felt they might get more status or a better job in another branch of the military. Navy recruiters appealed to men with promises of Pacific South Sea adventures. The air force promoted the idea of dramatic air combat by calling its pilots "Cowboys of the Sky." Leather flight jackets worn by pilots were considered emblems of courage. Other young men went for a stint in the marines, whose recruitment posters emphasized the appeal of marine uniforms to the opposite sex.

The new servicemen and women were everywhere—shuttling between training camps, shipping out for overseas, traveling home to families, or simply out on the town. In the two weeks following Pearl Harbor, U.S. railroads moved more than six-hundred thousand troops. People at train stations blended into monotones of army olive drab, navy blue, and marine green uniforms. The uniforms were known as "government issue," or GI. The hordes of men wearing them were also labeled GIs.

Before it was over, more than 16 million Americans wore a uniform in World War II, four times the number who served in the

A navy recruiting station is swamped with men waiting to volunteer for military service. More than sixteen million Americans would participate in the war.

first world war. At any given time, 12 million Americans were in the military—one out of every eleven citizens. Able-bodied men in civilian clothes became so scarce that the St. Louis Browns baseball team used a one-armed outfielder.

Draft Deferment

Although a great majority of Americans wanted to serve their country, some tried to avoid compulsory military service. The standard ways to avoid the draft were to claim conscientious objection, economic dependency of family or relatives, or employment in an essential occupation, such as farming or the defense industries. By 1944 over 2 million farmworkers were given occupational deferments because their work was essential to the national defense.

In the early years of the draft, men with children were excused from the draft. Babies were called "draft insurance," and in 1943 over 8 million fathers were deferred. But this changed as the war continued and the manpower dwindled on the battlefront.

By the end of 1944 only eighty-thousand fathers held deferments.

In view of the 50 million men who eventually registered, there were few who tried to evade the draft. Some men, however, tried to fake deafness, heart ailments, and mental disorders. Everett Stewart of Valley Station, Kentucky, could have won a prize for his attempts at draft evasion. Over the

Quickie Marriages

While some men married to stay out of the military service, those who were drafted were also in a marrying mood. Women flocked to soldiers, sailors, and marines; the marriage rate of women marrying servicemen soared to an estimated one thousand a day. The marriages acted as an anchor during the uncertainties of war.

Taboos of class, family consent, and courtships were swept aside. Some young people met and were married within days. Movie star–turned-private Mickey Rooney proposed marriage to a woman on his first date. The couple was married seven days later.

A few unscrupulous women married men only to receive the fifty dollars a month that was allotted to each serviceman's wife. These "Allotment Annies" were also the beneficiaries of the GIs' ten-thousand-dollar life-insurance policies. One Allotment Annie specialized in combat pilots, who were known to have high mortality rates. Others married more than one GI at a time.

Some wives traveled along with their husbands as the men were transferred from one U.S. military base to another. Women would be seen in crowded bus and train stations overloaded with suitcases and carrying crying babies. At each camp the women would set up housekeeping any way they could. Rents in nearby towns were often outrageous and conditions were deplorable. In some towns women paid up to fifty dollars a month to live in sheds and chicken coops in order to see their husbands a few hours a week. Other women were luckier and were able to stay with families who volunteered spare bedrooms in a time of need.

Wives of American soldiers gather outside a military-issue quonset hut. Some military wives were given temporary housing near their husbands.

course of several months, Stewart kept the local draft board posted on the alleged deterioration of his health by impersonating various family members. Stewart went to the draft board dressed as a sister, a half brother, and a crippled old uncle. Finally he reported his own death dressed as the grieving widow in a wig and floppy hat. This performance earned Stewart three years in a federal penitentiary.

Over 5 million men were rejected due to physical, educational, or mental problems. But physical requirements for the army were very low. A draftee only had to be five feet tall and weigh 105 pounds. He had to have correctable vision and at least half his natural teeth. He could not have flat feet, a hernia, or venereal disease. Even at those standards, about 50 percent of men were rejected. The chief causes of rejection—bad teeth and eyes—were a direct result of the recent Great Depression, when food and basic medical care was hard to find.

Illiteracy was also a problem. Over half a million men were rejected because they could not write their own names. By the end of the war, men were in such short supply that the army set up special schools to teach illiterates how to read and write at the fourth-grade level.

Conscientious Objectors

Most Americans who were qualified were ready to take up arms for the United States, a small percentage chose not to fight for reasons of conscience. About fifty thousand men were officially classified as conscientious objectors (COs) who would not fight due to religious or philosophical reasons. These COs were mainly Jehovah's Witnesses, Quakers, or Mennonites. Of these, about half agreed to enter the service as medics or in other jobs that would not require them to bear arms. Another twelve thousand performed nonmilitary service in the Civilian Public Service Camps.

Some nonreligious COs were political or philosophical pacifists. They were often college-educated, highly trained professionals such as teachers, social workers, and artists. Instead of fighting, some volunteered to be guinea pigs for testing new medicines. Others were forced to do manual labor such as digging ditches and cutting trees. They worked without wages and paid for their own food and clothing. Many resented the military regimen in the camps and organized strikes.

About six thousand of the men who refused to serve in any capacity were sent to federal prison; by 1944 one out of every six prisoners were COs. Using tactics that would later become popular in the civil rights movement, the COs sometimes staged work stoppages and hunger strikes to protest racial segregation, mail censorship, and other restrictions. In one prison a 135-day strike caused officials to integrate the dining halls. Prison officials, who dealt with hardened criminals, had never seen anything like it. One prison warden said he yearned "for the good old days of simple murderers and bank robbers."[6]

Meanwhile, the murderers could not understand the conscientious objectors. When one objector explained why he was in prison to a crime boss, the criminal answered, "You mean they put you in here for *not* killing?"[7]

You're in the Army Now

For the vast majority of American men, military service began when they gathered with another one hundred draftees at the local bus or train station. Each was allowed one suitcase and was often accompanied by a wife, girlfriend, or parents. In small towns, going-away parties were major events. High-school bands would play, the color guard from the local American Legion would march, and the marine hymn would be played while the entire town turned out for the send-off.

The men were taken to faraway training camps where they usually experienced culture shock and instant homesickness. Men from the North learned southern culture at Fort Benning, Georgia; Men from the South shivered in the cold at Camp McCoy, Wisconsin. College students had a particularly hard time in this world of foul language and country-and-western music. For the first six weeks in some camps the only book allowed was the Bible.

Once at the camp, the recruits got half-inch crewcuts, were vaccinated by doctors with inch-long needles, and were issued uniforms that rarely fit. The recruits gave up their identities for a rank and a serial number. They surrendered their freedom to mind-numbing, exhausting rituals of calisthenics, marching at 128 steps per minute, practicing with their weapons, and performing the drudgeries of kitchen work. The privates also learned a new language: Food was *chow*, moving fast was *on the double*, and *SNAFU* meant "situation normal, all fouled up."

Boot camp was eight hard weeks of training before a GI was shipped off to active duty. The sergeants and officers who presided over the fledgling soldiers were considered monsters. It seemed their only job was to make the men miserable. But GIs had to train under extremely rigorous

Men are vaccinated and given uniforms as part of their initiation into military service.

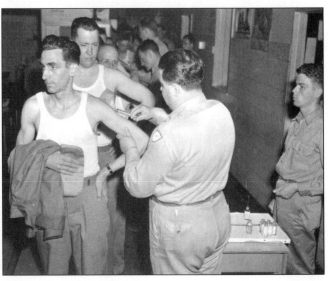

standards. The army's written requirements for each new soldier were detailed
in the book *G.I.* by Lee Kennett:

> The culmination of physical training
> was the requirement that the soldier
> with rifle and thirty pound pack, ne-
> gotiate a 1500 foot obstacle course in
> three and a half minutes. Specific re-
> quirements were that he take off with
> a yell (yelling or singing frequently
> accompanied physical activity),
> mount an eight foot wall, slide down
> a ten foot pole, leap a flaming trench,
> weave through a series of pickets,
> crawl through a water main, climb a
> ten foot rope, clamber over a five foot
> fence, swing by a rope across a seven
> foot ditch, mount a twelve foot ladder
> and descend to the other side, charge
> over a four foot breastwork [fortifica-
> tion], walk a twenty foot catwalk some
> twelve inches wide and seven feet over
> the ground, swing hand over hand
> along a five foot horizontal ladder,
> slither under a fence, climb another,
> and cross the finish line at a sprint.[8]

In the early days, there was a general
lack of military supplies. Ford trucks were
painted with signs that read TANK. What
tanks were available often broke down.
Major General George S. Patton Jr., who
began his military career as a commander
of an ill-equipped armored division, ordered parts for his broken tanks from
Sears & Roebuck catalogs and paid for
them out of his own pocket.

*As commander of an armored division, Major
General George S. Patton Jr. resorted to ordering
his military supplies from Sears & Roebuck.*

For all the early growing pains, the army
and its air force quickly became a modern
fighting force. In less than two years after
Pearl Harbor, the army grew from 300,000
men to 7.7 million men and women. The
number increased to 8.3 million by the end

of the war. In addition, there were 3.4 million men and women in the navy, 484,000 in the marines, and 170,000 in the Coast Guard.

Daily Life on the Base

Life did not get much easier for GIs after they were finished with boot camp. In the morning, troops were roused from bed at the crack of dawn by a bugler playing "Reveille." The day was spent marching, standing at rigid attention, and training. A great deal of nightlife was spent in barracks waiting to be called overseas. Some troublemakers might end up on KP (kitchen

A flood of soldiers gather during mail call. Often separated from their families for the first time, soldiers eagerly awaited news from home.

police) duty peeling potatoes all day. Others might end up in the stockade (jail).

Mail call was the highlight of the day. Letters, postcards, and care packages from home were eagerly awaited. Packages might include a mother's homemade cookies, a hand-knitted scarf, a shoeshine kit, a paperback book, a magazine, or a special photograph of a loved one. (One of the companies to benefit from loved ones writing to lonely GIs was the Parker Company, producers of pens and inks. The war effort boosted sales of Parker ink by 800 percent.) Soldiers also received a week or two of vacation—called a furlough—when they could return home to visit friends and family. These short reunions were filled with sentiment and precious memories. Once back at camp or shipped overseas, a soldier's last memory of home was often of his furlough.

Women Who Answered the Call

Men were not the only ones who answered America's call to arms. The Women's Army Corps (WACs) opened the doors to women in 1943. By the war's end, over 143,000 women would serve in the WACs. These women drove trucks, flew airplanes, operated control towers, repaired equipment, and mastered Morse code—in all, they performed more than 235 different army jobs.

Female recruiting began on May 27, 1943. College students, career women, secretaries, and housewives all applied for

A recruiting poster urges women to join the military. Many women responded to the call—143,000 would serve.

service. So great was the turnout in Washington, D.C. that embarrassed recruiters ran out of applications twice during the first day. In New York, fourteen hundred women stood in line for eight hours to sign up.

Like all recruits, the women endured ill-fitting uniforms and rigorous training. (They were issued regular GI clothing as well as two girdles and three brassieres each.) But the women also had to endure wisecracks and prejudice from male GIs who were unaccustomed to their presence in the military.

Women recruits underwent the same rigid regimen as the men. They were inspected by officers who scrutinized everything from their hairdos to the shine on their shoes. They sweated their way through gas-mask drills and marched cross country. Women dug slit trenches, bathed out of helmets, and clamored over obstacle courses.

The women and men who put on uniforms in World War II signified the largest call to war in U.S. history. Everyone who stayed behind knew someone who was fighting. But the war was not just being fought overseas—it was a war that would be won on the home front as well.

By the war's end, over three hundred thousand women would serve in the navy's Women Accepted for Volunteer Emergency Service (WAVES), the air force's Women's Auxiliary Ferrying Squadron (WAFS), the Women's Air Force Service Pilots (WASP), the marines, the WACs, and the Coast Guard.

Chapter 2

Bringing the War Home

In early 1942 the country's juke-boxes played hits such as "Good-bye Mama, I'm Off to Yokohama," and "You're a Sap, Mister Jap." But these were the dark days of the war. Japanese forces easily conquered Guam, Manila, Singapore, and Bataan.

Closer to home, America proved woefully unable to defend itself. In February, when a reporter asked Roosevelt whether the United States was open to enemy attack, the president said, "Enemy ships could swoop in and shell New York; enemy planes could drop bombs on war plants in Detroit; enemy troops could attack Alaska."[9] As if to confirm Roosevelt's gloomy statement, the first direct enemy attack on the continental United States occurred a few days later.

Fighting the War in America

On February 23, 1942, a lone Japanese submarine surfaced one mile offshore north of Santa Barbara, California, and began lobbing shells at an oil refinery. The shooting was not very effective—the sub fired twenty-five shells in twenty minutes but caused only minor damage.

Then, on September 9, 1942, a pontoon-equipped Japanese bomber flown by Nobuo Fujita was launched off the deck of a submarine near Oregon. Fujita navigated to shore using a lighthouse beacon that had not been blacked out and dropped two incendiary bombs on a forest region in Oregon.

The aim of the mission was to start a firestorm that would sweep down the coast; however, the flames sputtered out quickly in the damp forest. Fujita tried to start another forest fire on September 29. Again the forest refused to burn. The only enemy pilot to ever bomb the United States gave up and went home.

By 1944 Americans had grown blasé about the threat of enemy bombers, but the Japanese did manage to cause some casualties and damage on U.S. soil. These

Japanese flyer Nobuo Fujita dropped bombs onto a forest in Oregon, hoping to set off widespread forest fires. Fortunately, the forest refused to burn.

after they were dropped. The balloons were released from Japan to ride the high-velocity stratospheric air currents across the Pacific. Each balloon was cleverly designed to dip ground-ward, drop a single bomb, and soar up again to distribute the rest of the bombs further to the east.

About three hundred of the balloons reached the United States and Canada. Some of them sailed as far east as Iowa and Kansas. Most of the bombs failed to explode, but one had tragic consequences. The fatal bomb landed on Mount Gear-hart in Oregon. Reverend Archie Mitchell had taken his wife and five children to the mountain to camp. While Mitchell parked the car, the others searched for a campsite. On the way they came upon the bomb on the ground. It exploded and killed all six.

Most Americans had no knowledge of the balloon bombs until the war was over. The government clamped strict censorship on details of the event to prevent the Japanese from finding out that the balloons were effective. Unaware of their success, the Japanese abandoned the balloon project.

German submarines (U-boats) caused substantially more damage. The U-boats prowled unimpeded up and down the

bombs were carried not by airplanes but by thousands of large paper balloons. Each balloon carried several thirty-pound bombs timed to explode three to five days

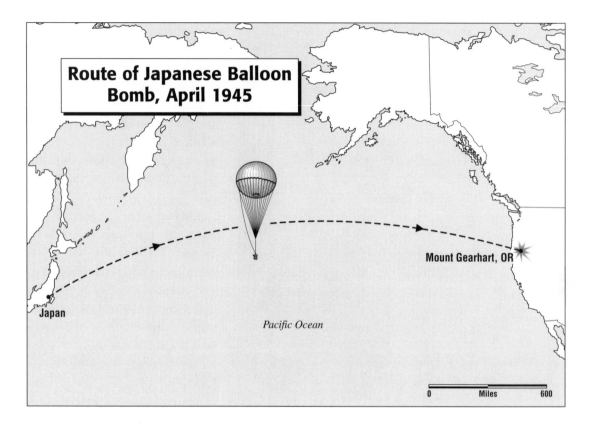

Route of Japanese Balloon Bomb, April 1945

Mount Gearhart, OR

Japan

Pacific Ocean

0   Miles   600

east coast from Canada to the Gulf of Mexico and into the Caribbean. They preyed on U.S. tankers and freighters sailing to Great Britain to supply that country with guns, tanks, and planes. From January to May 1942, eighty-seven ships were attacked and sunk in American waters.

The neon glow of Miami proved to be an inviting beacon to German U-boats. Week after week tourists on beaches could watch burning ships sink off the coast. Survivors of attacks staggered to shore as the navy erected fences to keep out the curious and prevent people from learning the full extent of the losses.

The navy and army air force hunted down U-boats in international waters off America's coast. But another branch of government, the Office of Civilian Defense (OCD), developed its own antisubmarine unit—the Civilian Air Patrol (CAP). Since younger men and women were needed for the military, CAP was formed by pilots who were too old to be drafted or were otherwise not eligible for service. CAP used forty thousand part-time pilots who served without pay. They flew their own light aircraft on missions that included ferrying military personnel and mail, and dropping mock bombs—

sacks filled with flour—to demonstrate the vulnerability of American factories to business owners and government officials.

In 1942 CAP airplanes were armed with real bombs as they undertook submarine patrols in the Atlantic. By 1943 CAP pilots successfully bombed fifty-seven German U-boats.

Civilian Defense

The emergency caused by World War II forced Americans to accept a level of regimentation and government interference in their lives that would never have been ac-

cepted in peacetime. The OCD, or Civilian Defense Corps (CD) as it was called, was formed seven months before Pearl Harbor. It was the main government agency in charge of civilians on the home front. The first director was the mayor of New York City, Fiorello H. LaGuardia. His assistant was the president's wife, Eleanor Roosevelt. LaGuardia coined a phrase when he called on Americans to contribute an "hour a day for the U.S.A."

The five-foot-two LaGuardia was a colorful character who often led New Yorkers on citywide air-raid drills complete

The Civilian Defense Corps, the agency that guided civilian war efforts on the home front, was directed by New York City Mayor Fiorello LaGuardia (left, holding poster) and assisted by the president's wife, Eleanor Roosevelt (below, with wounded soldier).

with mock fires, fake broken water mains, and make-believe accidents. On the day the Japanese attacked Pearl Harbor, he drove through the streets of New York in a siren-blaring police car yelling, "Calm! Calm! Calm!"[10] Two days later the mayor was on the west coast organizing civilian defense forces when a false report of approaching enemy planes led to an air-raid alert in New York. To LaGuardia's embarrassment, most New Yorkers paid no attention to the wailing sirens except to gaze up at the sky.

The job of the CD was to instruct Americans in activities that would protect their homes and families in the event of an air raid or other enemy attack. Over 12 million volunteers (almost as many as the armed forces) carried out Civilian Defense duties. Some of the positions within the CD were air-raid warden, plane spotter, messenger, auxiliary fireman, auxiliary policeman, fire watcher, member of the bomb squad, road repair crewman, member of the decontamination squad, and demolition crewman. Other citizens were part of the Emergency Food and Housing Corps, the Drivers Corps, the Medical Corps, or the Nurses' Aides Corps.

Practically every community in the United States was organized down to each city block. During air-raid drills, CD members wore white metal helmets and armbands and carried whistles around their necks. The wardens would be seen on the streets of darkened cities and towns making sure lights were out and blackout curtains were properly drawn in every house. After all-clear sirens were sounded, the CD volunteers would return home.

During the early days of the war there was an equipment shortage—some air-raid wardens had to use dime-store whistles marked Made in Japan. Other equipment shortages forced communities to patch together their own air-raid sirens. Reading, Pennsylvania, used dozens of automobile horns that blasted out the letter *V* (as in *victory*) in Morse code. In Sepulveda, California, a one-hundred-year-old bell acted as an alarm. The federal government finally

The Civilian Defense Corps recruited over 12 million volunteers. Almost every city block in the country had a CD organization.

awarded a contract to Bell Telephone Laboratories to develop a standard model siren. Bell's siren was powered by a car engine and was so loud it could be heard for ten square miles. It was said to rupture eardrums at a distance of one hundred feet. It was so loud that many cities refused to buy it, and the army considered using it as a weapon.

When no attacks materialized, some Americans began to resent blackouts. To others, however, it was a way to spend time in patriotic thought and to identify with the troops on the battlefront and in war-torn cities. Many people who were children at that time remember the excitement of sitting by dim candlelight and enjoying the mystery and sense of danger the blackout conveyed.

The Office of Civilian Defense was closed down late in 1943 after the threat of invasion in the United States seemed unlikely. Air-raid drills and blackout restrictions, however, remained in place for the duration.

Preparing for the Worst

Americans could take few precautions in the event of an air raid. Many cities kept boxes of sand and pails of water on street corners to put out fires, but a shortage of building materials prevented any large-scale construction of bomb shelters. The White House maintained a bomb shelter in the basement of the Treasury Building, but most other Americans were not so lucky. Still, people had to have somewhere to go

Dancing in Bomb Shelters

Besides planning for air raids, the Office of Civilian Defense was supposed to enroll civilians in community activities such as health, welfare, child care, and physical fitness programs. These activities were directed by the president's wife, Eleanor Roosevelt. Ronald H. Bailey describes the First Lady's efforts in *The Home Front, U.S.A.*

> Mrs. Roosevelt plunged into her new job with characteristic zeal. She proclaimed a national "Dance-for-Health-Week" and personally led lunch-hour folk dances in the corridors at OCD headquarters.
>
> She also made two appointments that quickly became centers of controversy. One was the actor Melvyn Douglas, an outspoken liberal, to head the division's Arts Council. The other was a ballroom dancer named Mayris Chayney, an old acquaintance of hers, to be chief of the Children's Activities Section of the Physical Fitness Division. . . . Miss Chayney's . . . new job was to develop programs of dancing and rhythmic exercises that could be performed in air-raid shelters. . . .
>
> The appointment of a dancer gave [Roosevelt's enemies in Congress] a field day—especially after they discovered that the Physical Fitness Division employed no fewer than 62 coordinators for such unwarlike sports as quoits, horseshoe pitching and table tennis. They mocked Mrs. Roosevelt's appointee as a "fan dancer" and "a strip teaser" and, in the unkindest cut of all to the First Lady, passed a rider to OCD's appropriations bill in February 1942 that prohibited the use of federal funds for "instruction in physical fitness by dancers, fan-dancing, street shows, theatrical performances or other public entertainment." Melvyn Douglas and Mayris Chayney resigned. So did Eleanor Roosevelt, probably to her husband's relief.

when air-raid sirens blasted. They were herded into doorways, under theater marquees, and into buildings designated with a yellow *S* (for *shelter*). For those caught on the street with nowhere to go, the CD advised "Cover your head and put your handkerchief between your teeth to keep them from being broken by bomb shock."[11]

The CD also advised citizens on proper behavior during an air raid by distributing 57 million pamphlets. They suggested that readers lie under a sturdy table when the bombs fell. The CD also advised people to learn first-aid training. Consequently, the best-selling book of 1942 was the *Red Cross First Aid Manual*, which sold 8 million copies. Volunteers practiced splinting and bandaging on spouses and children at home. Then, during air-raid drills, they would display their skill on mock victims—Boy Scouts splashed with ketchup to simulate blood.

Some of the advice given by CD officials turned out to be dangerous or harmful. For example, the CD board in New York told citizens to fill their wash basins and bathtubs with water in the event of an air raid. The reasoning was that the water could be used to fight fires. After several months, the board realized that if the sirens sounded and everyone started filling their bathtubs, there would be a considerable strain on the city's water pressure, causing fire hydrants to be useless. New recommendations advised citizens to keep a few gallons of water for drinking purposes.

Junior Commandos

Although they were thousands of miles from the battlefields, the war deeply touched American children. For many, their fathers were known only to them by a picture on the mantel. Likewise, their mothers were away at work for most of the day. Because of shortages, children could not get rubber balls, tricycles or doll carriages—all made from scarce war materials. At school, children regularly practiced air-raid drills in which they crouched under their desks or in windowless hallways.

But children pitched in with the same enthusiasm as their parents. Some made clothes for children in war-torn lands. Others knitted socks for GIs. Some collected milkweed pods—the fluffy seeds inside were used for life jackets. Kids also packed sacks with flour to make mock bombs used in air-raid drills. Most of these activities were channeled through youth organizations such as 4-H clubs, Boy Scouts, Girl Scouts, and the Junior Red Cross.

Comic-strip character Little Orphan Annie promoted an organization called Junior Commandos, which was modeled on the real army organization of captains, majors, and colonels. The commandos played war games and ran obstacle courses with wooden guns and tin helmets.

Children in a Seattle elementary school crouch below their school tables during an air-raid drill.

It was a matter of pride between cities to be first on the list of hypothetical targets for enemy bombers. Chicago published a pamphlet that showed it was closer to Germany, via the polar route, than German-occupied Norway was to New York. People who knew better pointed out that no land-based enemy planes could carry enough fuel to reach the United States from Europe and then return. But there was a fear that Axis pilots might drop bombs and then bail out of their planes by parachute. A *Colliers* magazine editorial pleaded with "any civilians who may reach these airmen ahead of the police or soldiers not to obey the human impulse to lynch them, shoot them, or kick them to death."[12] In fact, even one-way trips from enemy-occupied territory were not possible.

There was never any real threat of large-scale bombing of American cities during World War II. But in Hollywood, Warner Studio head Jack Warner was not taking any chances. The studios were practically next door to a prime potential target—the Lockheed Aircraft factory. Warner did not bother to build a bomb shelter, however. Instead, he had a twenty-foot-long arrow painted on the roof of a sound stage with a sign that read LOCKHEED THATAWAY.

Spies Among Us

Most Americans understood that the United States was safe from enemy bombs, but the threat of spies and espi-

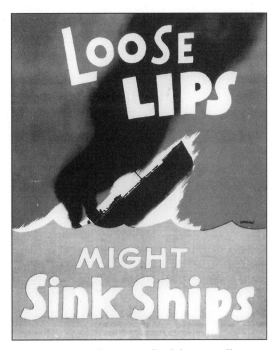

A poster warns that any talk of the war effort may lead to spies getting information that could be used to sink American ships.

onage was a clear and present danger. People who worked in defense-related industries worked under huge posters that read "Enemy agents are always near; if you don't talk, they won't hear," and "Loose Lips Sink Ships."[13] Likewise, newspapers urged readers to report suspicious people to the Federal Bureau of Investigation (FBI).

These suspicious characters were said to have been either enemy agents that sneaked into the United States or homegrown sympathizers, called "fifth columnists." The phrase originated in the

Spanish civil war when a general was taking over Madrid with four columns of soldiers. The general said he had a "fifth column" of sympathizers within the city.

During World War II the FBI investigated almost twenty thousand suspected cases of domestic sabotage but could not find one enemy to arrest. However, a daring sabotage attempt in 1942 proved, in the words of the day, it *could* happen here.

As dawn was breaking on June 13, the German U-boat *Innsbruck* surfaced a mere five hundred yards off Long Island, New York. Four men paddled to shore in a rubber raft. The Germans had lived in the United States before the war, spoke fluent English, and knew American customs and geography. They had also been trained at a special school for saboteurs in Berlin, Germany. A similar team landed in Florida four days later.

The two teams had explosives and incendiaries (devices that cause extremely hot fires) and were supposed to conduct a two-year campaign of sabotage against American war industries. Their targets were aluminum plants, rail lines, and dams and locks on the Ohio River.

The deadly mission of sabotage quickly unraveled. The men on Long Island had evaded the navy but landed only half a mile from a Coast Guard station. As the saboteurs were changing into civilian clothes, an unarmed Coast Guardsman literally caught them with their pants down. The Coast Guardsman heard one of the men speaking German, but he pre-

tended that the spies were lost American fishermen. The Guardsman forced three hundred dollars on the saboteurs, told them to have a good time, and left. A Coast Guard search party soon returned to the site and found the explosives the saboteurs had hastily buried.

Meanwhile, the Germans had blundered through a nearby trailer park to a local train station. They took the train to Manhattan, bought new clothes on Fifth Avenue, dined at a restaurant, and were overheard talking loudly about their mission.

In the meantime, the team in Florida had split into two groups. One pair went to New York by train, the other went to Chicago to visit relatives and await further orders. Within two weeks, however, the FBI had enough evidence to capture both spy teams.

The eight saboteurs were tried immediately in total secrecy before a military commission. All were sentenced to death, but Roosevelt commuted the sentences to thirty years for the two men who had cooperated with the FBI. The two were released after five years, and the rest were sent to the electric chair. Roosevelt later said that his only regret was that the saboteurs were not hanged—a punishment he felt was more fitting.

Paying the Ultimate Cost of Freedom

While Americans were undergoing a few physical hardships, the real hardships were the constant worries and concerns for loved

Laughing at the Enemy

While the government tried to instill hatred for Japanese, German, and Italian leaders, Americans turned Tojo, Hitler, and Mussolini into jokes. Hitler was the first to be parodied. While he was feared and hated in Europe, American caricatures made fun of Hitler's trademark little black mustache; dark, brooding eyes; and haircut with the bangs falling over half his forehead. He was portrayed as a wolf, a pig, a skunk, and a chicken. The goose-stepping Nazis, with one arm raised in salute, were also the butt of jokes.

These caricatures appeared everywhere from magazine articles and posters to dolls, dart boards, and piggy banks. An ashtray portrayed a skunk with Hitler's face. The caption below read, "Jam your cigarette butts on this skunk." A ceramic Hitler doll, which had its posterior turned into a pincushion, read: "It is good luck to find a pin—here's an Axis to stick it in."

As the war heated up, Mussolini and Tojo joined this comic parade. Wartime gift and novelty shops carried these items, or they could be won as prizes in amusement arcades. They were also re-created on war posters that hung in schools, factories, and training camps.

THEY'RE WATCHING US... *PLENTY!*

THE STUFF "ON ORDER" DOESN'T COUNT... BUT REAL PRODUCTION HURTS THEM!

PUT *ALL* YOUR POWER IN THE JOB!

DODGE

Caricatures of Mussolini, Hitler, and Tojo spy from a war poster asking American workers to increase their productivity.

ones overseas. This brought the anguish and tragedy of World War II to the home front more than any saboteurs or balloon attacks could. War may not have devastated the United States the way it did other countries, but the loss of a son or husband was the ultimate hardship. And something from which some people never recovered.

In *Americans Remember the Home Front,* the editor of *Newsday* magazine talks about his difficult job:

The most popular feature on the paper, which almost broke your heart, were the casualty lists—every day a new casualty list. And often you had to send reporters to families who had just received the news that their son was lying on some beach, or whatever. It was a tragic period, and it did get to you. I hated to read those casualty lists for fear of finding friends on it. And you often did.[14]

In the same book a grieving mother, Betty Brice, remembers her son Dalton:

Dalton was eighteen years old and valedictorian of his class. He had an American Legion scholarship, but he went down and applied for immediate induction as soon as he graduated from high school. He went overseas—I think he was gone seven months from the time he enlisted.

I was out raking the yard when I got the telegram. The man who brought it went next door to my neighbor and asked if she would come over with him, because it was the third one he had delivered that day in our town. When he handed me the telegram, I just looked at it. He said, "It's bad news." I guess I was kind of in a state of shock, until I read it, you know, seeing he's gone, that was it. The police went

Mrs. Thomas F. Sullivan learns that all five of her sons were killed when their ship was sunk by the Japanese.

to the high school and brought my younger son, Kenny, home. We had a terrible time getting him calmed down, and of course, my ten-year-old daughter took it awfully hard.

Dalton was home once after he went in. I knew, when I put him on the bus, I'd never see him again; I just had this feeling. And while he was home, he got rid of everything in the house that belonged to him. He must have had a feeling too. He received the Silver Star, and there was a citation that came with it which told about it. They were in Germany, six miles past the Remagen bridge. He was a medic; he went to help some fellows in a burning tank and was killed by a sniper on his way back. It took me about a year before I could really get a hold of myself. I think I cried day and night for three or four months. It was a terrible thing to happen to anyone. He was so young.[15]

Chapter 3

Family Life During the War

Daily life in America changed drastically during the war. While workers might have gotten up a 7:00 A.M. before, the wartime alarm went off at 6:00 A.M. With gas and oil shortages, commuters could no longer use their private cars—they had to get up earlier to use jam-packed buses, trolleys, and commuter trains.

A Different Style at Work

Traditional work rules were relaxed and camaraderie flourished in factories and offices. People pulled together and problems such as loafing and office politics seemed foolish and irrelevant while soldiers were dying overseas. With labor shortages, forty-eight-hour work weeks were the rule, and that was often exceeded to meet production quotas handed down from the government.

Clothing shortages meant that women could no longer buy new dresses when necessary, and this meant they could come to work in pants for the first

time. To save cloth, the skirts that were manufactured ended an inch above the knee—by government order. With all the wool being used for military uniforms, prized sweaters or suits were not used for everyday wear.

Two-piece swimsuits also became fashionable. When nylon and silk stockings were no longer available, women wore "bottled stockings," in which they painted seams down the backs of their legs with eyebrow pencils, or put makeup on their legs to simulate the color of stockings.

Men wore "victory suits," which saved cloth because they had narrow lapels, short jackets, and no vests or cuffs.

After a hard day, when children were fed supper and put to bed, the adults could finally sit down and rest—in a living room made gloomy by blackout curtains and chilled by a thermostat set no higher than sixty-five degrees Fahrenheit. Adults might play cards or board games and listen to the radio. Going out to a movie was possible if

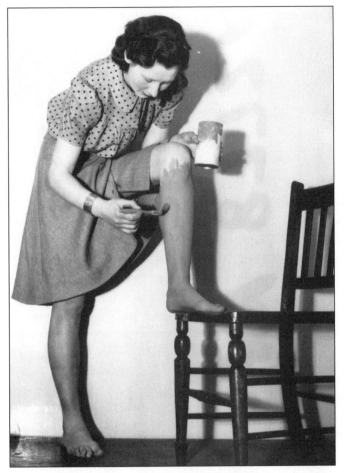

A woman copes with war shortages of nylon by painting her legs to simulate stockings.

personal contribution to the war effort. And that gave their lives a sense of purpose and direction as never before.

Food Rationing

With millions of soldiers to feed overseas, Americans at home were forced to deal with food shortages on a daily basis. In the morning, the traditional American breakfast of eggs, bacon, toast, and coffee changed dramatically. Eggs were plentiful, but bacon was rationed and could only be purchased with meat-ration stamps that were doled out by the government. There was less butter to be slathered on the toast and less sugar to put in the coffee, which itself was now in short supply. (Ships that brought coffee in from South America were diverted for military purposes.)

it was within walking distance. Otherwise precious gasoline would have to be used.

Life on the home front was a constant barrage of shortages, disruptions, and inconveniences. People might have been annoyed, but after all, everyone else was enduring the same conditions. Many Americans felt that their coping was a

Sugar was the first item to be rationed in 1942. Americans lined up at their local elementary schools, and teachers asked them how much sugar they already had at home. Ration books were then issued for a fifty-two-week supply. The *Ladies' Home Journal* of July 1942 explained to readers why sugar had to be rationed: "Sugar cane is needed to make molasses. Molasses is used to make industrial alcohol which is need to make explosives. Explosives are needed to sink the Axis!"[16]

In 1943 processed foods such as soups, canned juices, and canned vegetables were added to the ration list. This was followed by meat, fish, and dairy rationing. Dealing with ration coupons and food shortages was often a complicated and frustrating experience.

Every American was issued two ration books from the Office of Price Administration (OPA), the government office in charge of rationing. Ration books were filled with sheets of perforated stamps. One contained blue coupons for canned goods, the other had red coupons for meat, fish, and dairy products. Every person was allowed forty-eight blue points and sixty-eight red points per month. A housewife with three children, in this case, had a total of 192 points to buy canned goods. At the start of every new month, everyone got new coupons and new numbers to juggle. To prevent hoarding, stamps were coded to be redeemable for only one month.

Points were given to specific items depending on their availability. Goods in the stores were marked with prices as well as how many points they were worth. Applesauce might take up ten points in March 1943 and climb to twenty-five points a year later. Grapefruit juice might drop from twenty-three points to four in the same period. In September 1943 a rib-eye steak was worth twelve points and hamburger seven. Lard was worth three points, butter sixteen. A bottle of tomato ketchup was worth fifteen points, and a forty-six-ounce can of pineapple juice was worth twenty-two.

On the average, each American was allowed about two pounds of meat per week. In some parts of the country meat shortages forced the government to institute "meatless Tuesdays." When a large shipment of rationed meat was made available, rumors quickly spread and long lines formed outside of butcher shops.

Liquor was hard to get and this led to bootleggers brewing their own whiskey—which sometimes proved to be lethal. As in other times of great stress, large segments of the population

Examples of World War II-era ration books. All food was rationed to maximize the amount of food that could be shipped overseas to feed soldiers.

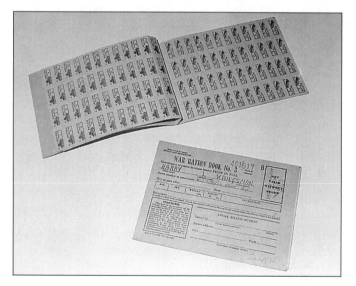

The Golden Rule of Food Rationing

The Office of Price Administration issued ration books to millions of citizens. The stamps inside were used to buy gas, sugar, meat, and canned and dairy goods. Handy hints for using ration stamps were printed everywhere. The example below is "The Golden Rule of Food Rationing" from the *Victory Cookbook,* reprinted in Robert Heidé and John Gilman's *Home Front America.*

[1] Share your food with our fighting men.

[2] Shop early in the day, early in the week, to lighten congestion at the store.

[3] Make up a shopping list and add up the points BEFORE you shop. Include fresh fruits and vegetables, cereals, and other unrationed foods where you can.

[4] Plan your family diet carefully. Get enough nourishment. Make up your menus for the week.

[5] Use 8- and 5-point stamps when you can, save 1- and 2-point stamps to make the count come out even. Your grocer cannot give you change in Blue Stamps.

[6] Do all the home canning possible.

[7] Don't blame your grocer for wartime inconvenience.

A woman uses ration stamps to purchase food at her local grocery.

drank heavily. Consumption of hard alcohol increased by 30 percent.

Victory Gardens

Secretary of Agriculture Claude R. Wickard came up with the idea of "victory gardens" soon after Pearl Harbor. These small gardens were encouraged by the government even though American farmers were already growing enough food to feed half the world.

Millions of gardens in small backyards and on city rooftops sprouted up across the country overnight. Crowded neighborhoods turned vacant lots into community gardens, where people took turns

A vegetable garden carries a sign that proclaims it to be a "Victory Garden." Such gardens were planted in a patriotic effort to increase the amount of food produced.

set aside at least one acre of land to grow vegetables for their own families or to sell at low prices at roadside stands.

Victory gardens sprang up in the most unlikely of places. There were "V gardens" in the Portland, Oregon, zoo; at Chicago's Arlington Race Track; and in downtown parking lots in New Orleans.

The U.S. Department of Agriculture distributed information about growing victory gardens. Other publishers printed books with titles such as *Food Gardens for Defense, Gardening for Victory,* and *Grow Your Own Food and Feed Your Family.* Dozens of magazines and posters encouraged Americans to plant victory gardens. The books coached beginners on the fine arts of plowing, raking, watering, and weeding. They counseled people on ridding their gardens of aphids, caterpillars, cabbage worms, and Japanese beetles, which were annihilated with a special vengeance. Gardeners were advised to put up scarecrows to frighten off crows and jay birds, and some of these were fashioned to look like Hitler or Mussolini.

Even movie magazines got in on the trend. One featured the glamorous actress Joan Crawford hard at work weeding her victory garden. (Crawford, it was reported,

planting, weeding, and watering. Extra food was donated to the needy. Those who owned farms were required by law to liked to grow beets, cauliflower, carrots, and squash. She had a special section devoted to red, yellow, and white tomatoes.)

During the peak war years, about 20.5 million victory gardens were planted in America that produced well over one-third of the vegetables in the country. Vegetables not immediately consumed were preserved in glass mason jars. These jars were packed with produce and sealed with metal lids and rubber rings.

First-time gardeners quickly found out how much work and attention a vegetable garden requires. But these gardens allowed a family to save money and fulfill their patriotic duty at the same time.

Wartime Cooking

Home-front cooks during World War II faced a daunting task when planning menus. In 1944 *Woman's Day* magazine offered a three-page section called "Wartime Cooking." A week of low-cost menus was offered for a family of four. The cost

Children in New Jersey tend a Victory Garden at their school in 1940. Children were encouraged to help on the home front.

for breakfast, lunch, and dinner for one week amounted to thirteen dollars. According to *Home Front America,*

> Some of the items featured for dinner were a liver-and-sausage loaf (55¢), quick tomato cheese puffs (29¢), and stuffed breast of veal (89¢). Steak, bacon, or prime meats were noticeably absent from the magazine's wartime weekly plan. Coffee was suggested for the adults while children got milk. Desserts like Indian pudding, butterscotch pudding and Norwegian prune pudding, were all made from a pre-mixed and boxed product.[17]

A *Good Housekeeping* magazine from 1942 suggests spaghetti and thinly cut pork chops served in a casserole with canned peas or buttered broccoli on the side. Spicy sauces or garnishes such as pineapple slices were recommended to take the focus off the bland wartime menu. Baked meatloaf became a standard dish as did canned baked beans served with the George A. Hormel Company's "spiced ham" product called Spam.

Since Spam required no refrigeration and was not rationed as beef was, it became a prime staple in American meals. Using ads placed in women's magazines, Hormel encouraged home-front housewives to serve Spam in a variety of interesting ways. Some of these recipes included Spam with canned Spanish rice, Spam fried in Crisco and served with creamed corn or potato salad, Spam-

wiches with Spam, pickles, and mustard on bread, and Spam "Aloha" served with sliced pineapple and avocado. Leftovers were never thrown out. The next day, the

Winning the War with Chewing Gum

Many companies were forced to stop making peacetime consumer goods in order to produce war materials. Others had to convince the government that their peacetime product was also essential to the war effort. One such product was Wrigley chewing gum.

Philip K. Wrigley had to solve two large problems to stay in business. One was the lack of chicle, which, like rubber, had been coming from trees in Japanese-occupied Southeast Asia. The other problem was that chewing gum is half sugar, which was strictly rationed. Wrigley solved his first problem by importing chicle from South America. He brought his chicle in on boats carrying high-priority rubber to speed up the process.

To obtain sugar, Wrigley had to convince the government that his chewing gum was essential to the war effort. He argued that gum was a great reliever of wartime stress and that it slaked a soldier's thirst, kept his mouth moist, and could be substituted for tobacco when smoking was prohibited. He even claimed his sugar-laden product helped keep teeth clean. Wrigley ended up supplying a stick of gum in every package of army K (combat) rations—and also wound up packaging the rations at his factory.

Wrigley's gum thus became—along with cigarettes and Coca-Cola—the common currency for barter among GIs on foreign soil. Wrigley also sold his gum to defense plants with the sales pitch: "To help your workers feel better, work better, just see that they get five sticks of chewing gum every day."

food scraps turned up as hash, usually served with home fries, macaroni, or rice.

Pulling the Fat from the Fire

The War Production Board told housewives to save their meat fat after cooking so that it could be used to make explosives. Millions of cooks were glad to comply with this simple task in order to help the war effort. To promote this idea, a popular singer, Mildred Bailey, recorded a song called "Scrap Your Fat," which was often played on the radio. A wartime bulletin handed out to butcher shops details the reasons for fat recycling. It was reprinted in Robert Heide and John Gilman's *Home Front America:*

A woman turns in food fats that she has collected to help the war effort. Fat was boiled to make glycerin, which was used in the manufacture of explosives.

> THE NEED IS URGENT—The war in the Pacific has greatly reduced our supply of vegetable fats from the Far East. It is necessary to find substitutes for them. Fat makes glycerin. And glycerin makes explosives for us and our Allies—explosives to down Axis planes, stop their tanks, and sink their ships. We need millions of pounds of glycerin and you housewives can help supply it.[18]

Butcher shops offered two red ration points for every pound of fat brought in.

Liberty magazine ran an advertisement to induce housewives and restaurants to recycle fats. Actress Helen Hayes was shown pouring bacon fat into a can while two handsome sailors watched. She is quoted as saying,

> I'm told that a single pound of kitchen grease will make two anti-aircraft shells. So you can bet that not

one drop of waste fat in my house ever goes down the drain. Instead I send it back to my meat dealer—and on its way to war. I'm making it a wartime habit—are you?[19]

Another ad showed the actress—wearing glamorous white gloves—handing a large tin of fat to a beaming butcher.

Automobile, Rubber, and Gas Shortages

America's heavy industry was busy turning out machine guns, tanks, and airplanes. Meanwhile, over three hundred common consumer items were banned from production. These included bicycles, waffle irons, beer cans, toothpaste tubes, coat hangers—even metal caskets. But the most obvious blow to American consumers was the ban on new automobiles.

The last car made for civilian use in the United States rolled off the assembly lines in February 1942. It was a gray Pontiac with "blackout" trim substituted for chrome. By that time, Ford, Plymouth, Studebaker, and Packard had ended civilian production.

Two months after the last car was produced, the first gasoline shortages hit the east coast. By mid-May over 8 million motorists were forced to register for gas ration cards. The OPA declared in January 1943 that pleasure driving was banned for the duration of the war.

The OPA decided how much a person needed to drive on a case-by-case basis. Windshield stickers were lettered from A to X and were color coded. Each had its own designation that marked the car's allowable use. Category A was for pleasure driving only—good for three to five gallons of gas per week. Category B was for commuters who drove to work. Category C was for salespeople, deliveries, and other work-re-

Men wait in line to receive gas rationing stamps. Gas stamps were issued on a case-by-case basis.

lated driving. Category E was for emergency vehicles driven by clergy, police, firefighters, press photographers, and journalists. Category T was for truckers. The letter *X* was reserved for congressmen and required no rationing at all. This led to widespread criticism.

Each month some 3 billion gas stamps, each less than a square inch in size, changed hands. The consumer passed the stamps to the gas retailer, who gave them to the wholesaler, who gave them to the manufacturer, who had to account for them to the federal government. The OPA operated fifty-five hundred local rationing boards made up of volunteers to keep track of all the paperwork. It also employed sixty thousand full-time workers.

Gasoline and oil products were rationed because of tire shortages that were created when the supply of rubber was disrupted from the Dutch East Indies. Since driving wore out rubber tires, the government was forced to lower the speed limit on all highways to thirty-five miles per hour. Road signs that read Victory Speed 35 reminded drivers to slow down.

Millions of old tires were collected in rubber scrap drives. Worn automobile tires that were still usable had to be "recapped" with new treads again and again. In this process, a new tread was laid over the old sidewall of the tire. Sidewalls could not be recapped, so the tire was

Thousands of tires await recycling for the war effort. Numerous scrap drives urged Americans to turn in everything from cans to silk stockings.

thrown away once the sidewall wore out.

A slogan from a used-car dealer stated, "Your automobile is a weapon of war—it is your duty to keep it constantly in shape to serve your country's wartime transportation system."[20]

The rubber shortage affected more than car tires. Women soon found that production would stop on girdles, bathing suits, garters, corsets, and dozens of other clothing items that relied on elastic.

Scrap Drives

Building war tanks, planes, and bombs created shortages of tin, aluminum, and other metals. Citizens were urged to recycle their cans and foil. Scrap drives collected vast amounts of old car fenders, metal bars, old pipes, barrels, and other waste. (Antique car collectors in modern times sometimes lament the lack of pre–World War II cars and parts. Millions of the now-vintage autos were melted down for the war effort.)

Nylon and silk stockings were also turned in at salvage drives. Department stores, schools, offices, and factories set up large barrels to collect old stockings, blouses, and scarves. The silk was reprocessed into parachutes while the nylon was used for tow ropes, powder bags

Actress Rita Hayworth donated the bumpers from her car to a scrap drive.

for naval guns, and other items.

Civilian Defense (CD) volunteers played an important role in the home front's great scavenger hunt. Every community had a scrap drive of some sort during the entire war. Very little escaped the scavenger's net. In Boston, a black-tie event to benefit scrap drives brought in a Civil War–era Gatling gun as well as the governor's exercise machine. In Wyoming, a group took apart an old twenty-ton steam engine and had to build several miles of new road to get it to the scrap collection center. In a variation of Frank Loesser's Pearl Harbor fight song "Praise the Lord and Pass the Ammunition," old jalopies sprouted signs that read "Praise the Lord, I'll Soon Be Ammunition."

CD workers promoted scrap drives with examples of what could be done with the materials. One old shovel, for instance, could make four hand grenades. By the end of the war, scrap was supplying much of the steel and half the tin needed for American weapons production. Perhaps just as important, the collection drives joined home-front citizens in a common cause and helped boost morale.

The Black Market

The Office of Price Administration was everyone's favorite scapegoat. The rationing it controlled created resentment and frustration among the populace. Citizens took great delight in blunders

Kids Helping with Scrap Drives

Children were expected to help with the war effort when it came to scrap drives. Old metal toy cars and trucks went into the scrap heap along with Superman and Captain Marvel comic books. In 1942 the president himself sent out an appeal to Boy Scout and Girl Scout troops. It was reprinted in *Home Front America*.

> Boys and girls of America can perform a great patriotic service for their country by helping our National Salvage effort. Millions of young Americans turning their energies to collecting all sorts of scrap, metals, rubber, and rags can help turn the tide in our ever increasing war effort. They will earn the gratitude of every one of our fighting men by helping them get the weapons they need—now! I know they will do their part.

Children proved to be the most zealous collectors of scrap. They knocked on neighborhood doors to collect worn rubber overshoes and tin cans. Kids carefully peeled bits of foil off of cigarette packs and gum wrappers. The foil was rolled into balls worth fifty cents each. One youngster in Illinois collected more than one hundred tons of used paper and cardboard during the course of the war.

Salvage yards in every neighborhood were crowded with children delivering goods to help win the war. Often they were wearing government-issued banners that read, Slap the Jap Right off the Map by Salvaging Scrap!

Proud children pose with the efforts of their scrap metal drive. Such metal would be recycled into steel for war weapons.

created by the agency, such as the Philadelphia OPA office that failed to ration sufficient heating fuel for itself and had to shut down temporarily.

While most Americans only grumbled about the OPA, millions of others participated in illegal black markets in meat, gas, and other rationed goods. The consumer could have all these things if he or she was willing to pay "Mr. Black," as illegal sellers were called. People were charged two to three times the going price for such luxuries as nylon stockings and boneless ham.

Organized crime oversaw most of the black market. Criminals printed counterfeit ration stamps by the millions. The government tried to outwit them by printing the stamps on a special paper that would change color under ultraviolet light, but the racketeers simply stole the special paper from federal warehouses.

Even some local businesses dabbled in the black market. Longtime customers might be able to buy a pound of steak, a can of vegetables, or even a coveted chunk of bubble gum from "Mr. Black." Although there was stigma attached to cheating, rationing was so unpopular that many people looked the other way.

One estimate said that black-market purchases accounted for 25 percent of all retail business on the home front. Courts usually doled out only small fines to people caught selling on the black market.

The Positive Side of Shortages

Material shortages spurred creative research by scientists searching for substitutes and alternatives to common items. Newly invented plastics replaced hard-to-find rubber and metals. Pocket-sized paperback books replaced hardcover books. Vegetable margarine supplanted butter. For the most part, Americans accepted their sacrifices as badges of honor that united the nation in a patriotic cause.

Chapter 4

The Arsenal of Democracy

By 1943 industrial America had the machine power for an all-out war against Japan and Germany. It had the raw materials to feed the machines, willing workers to run them, and billions of dollars to pay for them.

America's role as the largest military producer in the world began the year before the attack on Pearl Harbor. In a speech calling for America to supply its allies—and build up its own defenses—President Roosevelt said, "We must be the great arsenal of democracy." [21]

It was a massive undertaking to change America's industrial focus from consumer goods to war output. Only the government could set priorities, award contracts, and divert natural resources for the effort. But businessmen—accustomed to freewheeling American capitalism—did not appreciate "government meddling" from Washington bureaucrats. They were also opposed to the regulations and huge amounts of paperwork that accompanied the task.

The government solved this problem using the "carrot-and-stick" approach. The "stick" was to deny uncooperative industries

Secretary of War Henry Stimson understood that American business would not support the Arsenal of Democracy unless it were allowed to make a profit.

raw materials such as steel and aluminum. The "carrot" was the massive profits that were gleaned from government contracts. Secretary of War Henry Stimson put it plainly in his diary, "If you are going to try to go to war, or to prepare for war, in a capitalist country, you have to let business make money out of the process or business won't work."[22]

Many small-business owners tried to get government contracts but failed. The maze of regulations, agencies, and divided authorities left many small businessmen out of the loop. Industrial giants fared much

better. A survey conducted in December 1942 showed that 71 percent of all defense contracts were held by America's one hundred biggest corporations.

Paying for the War with War Bonds

The entire financial cost of World War II to the United States was mind-boggling—more than $330 billion over a four-year

Franklin Roosevelt is photographed buying the first defense savings bond. By issuing the bonds, the government was able to raise money for the war.

period (this would be equal to tens of trillions of today's dollars). The government needed to pay for guns, bombs, bullets, tanks, planes, ships, and soldiers. To do this, it instituted a 5 percent surcharge on all income taxes—called a "victory tax" to justify the increase.

The government also began—for the first time—to automatically deduct a percentage of taxes from most Americans' paychecks. This was the beginning of the withholding tax that is deducted from paychecks of American wage earners to this day. This plan provided a large infusion of money into the U.S. Treasury and greatly reduced the number of people cheating on their taxes. To gain support for the deduction, billboards across the country urged "Pay Your Taxes, Beat the Axis."[23]

The Treasury's other great source of revenue was defense bonds or war bonds. Bonds were sold in denominations of $25 to $10,000, and Americans purchased more than $135 billion in war bonds during the war. Banks, insurance companies, and big corporations accounted for $99 billion of the total, but $37 billion was in small-denomination "E" bonds bought by ordinary citizens.

The first war bond was sold to Roosevelt on May 1, 1942, for $375; it would be worth $500 in ten years. A war bond was like a loan to the government. A $25 bond was sold for $18.75. A $100 bond cost $75. A $1,000 bond cost $750. If the bonds were not cashed in within the ten-year maturation period, the interest would continue to accumulate.

Victory-loan drives and war-bond rallies were held everywhere. Bonds were sold from booths on street corners and from post offices, banks, department stores, movie theaters, factories, and grocery stores. The American Women's Voluntary Services helped schools, churches, and other groups host war bond dances. These patriotic events would often take place on holidays such as St. Valentine's Day, St. Patrick's Day, and Christmas.

Children would do their part by purchasing ten-cent and twenty-five-cent defense stamps to paste in booklets. When a booklet was filled with stamps, the child would get his or her very own war bond. In 1944 alone, school sales of bonds and stamps paid for 11,700 parachutes, 2,900 planes, and more than 44,000 jeeps for the armed forces.

To sell the bonds, Secretary of the Treasury Henry Morgenthau solicited help from Madison Avenue advertising executives, comic-book heroes, and Hollywood movie stars. War-bond posters issued by the U.S. government contained slogans like Back the Attack. Others used scare tactics. One poster pictured three young girls being leered at by Nazi officers. Messages to buy war bonds soon appeared in magazines and on book covers, matchbooks, sheet music, and candy wrappers.

Actor James Cagney toured sixteen cities in three weeks leading a victory-loan show. Kate Smith, who sang "God Bless

BUY BONDS AT YOUR NEAREST SKOURAS THEATRE!

WHAT D'YA MEAN—
YOU AIN'T GONNA BUY NO BONDS!

Secretary of the Treasury Henry Morgenthau asked Madison Avenue advertising executives to come up with ideas such as this humorous poster to help sell bonds.

Betty Grable, and Dorothy Lamour. The Hollywood Bond Cavalcade featured a number of stars who raised $1 billion in ten cities in just one month. Carole Lombard, an energetic war-bond seller was tragically killed in a plane crash when returning home from a war-bond rally. She was viewed as a civilian war casualty by her adoring public.

To show the progress of the war-bond drive, a four-story-high cash register was set up in New York's Times Square to record the dollars and cents collected throughout the nation. By 1945, 85 million people, more than half the population of the United States, held war bonds.

Building B-24 Liberator Bombers

The U.S. government began building up its defense force in March 1941, when bulldozers began clearing sixty-seven acres of woods twenty-seven miles west of downtown Detroit, Michigan. The area was to be the site of the $65-million Willow Run plant owned and operated by Ford Motor Company. (The cost was underwritten by U.S. government bonds.) When completed, the factory—nearly a quarter-mile wide and half a mile long—was described as "the most enormous room in the history of man."[24] It was so large that cross-

America" thousands of times throughout the war to both soldiers and civilians, raised $40 million in one sixteen-hour radio marathon.

Other movie stars who lent Uncle Sam a hand were Lana Turner, Marlene Dietrich, factory errands had to be run by motor-cycle or car.

Willow Run was the largest aircraft factory in the world. It was designed to produce the B-24 Liberator long-range bombers at the rate of one per hour. The factory was set up so that raw materials were fed into one end of the building, and components were made in adjacent areas and joined together on four main assembly lines. The bombers converged on one line at the other end of the fac-tory, where they were rolled out onto concrete runways and flown off into the sky.

This complicated operation was plagued by problems from the start. A B-24 had about one hundred thousand parts compared to fifteen thousand parts

The interior of Willow Run—the largest aircraft factory in the world. The plant was originally plagued with high absenteeism and organization problems.

The Jeep and the Duck

World War II gave America two new vehicles that were to become legend by war's end. The first was the jeep—made by Willys-Overland and Ford—which proved as nimble as a motorcycle and as tough as a tank. Although some people claimed the name came from the odd animal character in the *Popeye* comic strip, the government claimed that it was a corruption of the official designation *GP*, meaning "general purposes." Whatever the case, the four-wheel-drive jeep could climb rocky hills, cross muddy swamps, and traverse sandy beaches. Although they were originally designed for messenger services, jeeps were soon used in every theater of war. When towing antitank guns they could quickly deliver firepower to bear on enemy armor. With a trailer attached, jeeps could evacuate wounded and dead. Jeeps were called "Iron Ponies," "Leaping Lenas," "Rough Riders," and "Panzer Killers."

The jeep's lesser-known cousin was the half-boat/half-truck DUK-W, or duck. The duck consisted of a boat body that encased a two-and-a-half ton truck chassis. The watertight hull was fitted with both a propeller and a rudder. Ducks were at home on the land or in the water. They were largely used for landing operations.

Transport ships would anchor in the water out of the range of enemy fire, open their bows, and disgorge hundreds of DUK-Ws into the water—each containing fifty soldiers. The ducks ferried troops and cargo ashore at speeds of up to 6.4 miles per hour and then drove them inland at speeds of up to 50 miles per hour. About one thousand ducks helped with the invasion of Sicily in 1943, and about two thousand were at the Normandy landing the following year.

Troops prepare for an amphibious landing in a DUK-W, or duck, in 1942.

in a typical Ford automobile. The first year the plant was in operation, the army air force ordered 575 major design changes. Each change required retooling of machines. Labor shortages created an even greater problem.

The plant was built before gasoline and tire rationing had been instituted. There was little housing in the immediate area, so most workers had to drive one hour each way from Detroit. With gas rationing restricted to only three to five gallons per week, the absentee rate for plant employees was astounding. During one month Willow Run hired twenty-nine hundred workers and lost thirty-one hundred. The company's seventy-nine-year-old founder, Henry Ford, did not help matters. He refused to allow union organizing, banned smoking on company time, and refused to hire women.

By 1943 Ford had relaxed his rules, but even then the plant was only making one B-24 a day. People across the country joked that Willow Run's name should have been "Willit Run?" The government forced Ford to decentralize the operation and make the aircraft parts at other Ford plants. This worked, and by 1944 Willow Run was rolling out one B-24 every sixty-three minutes. By the war's end, the plant produced 8,685 Liberators, each capable of delivering four tons of bombs apiece each time it flew over enemy territory.

Avalanche of Aircraft

The bombers that flew out of Willow Run were only a small part of the avalanche of aircraft produced by Detroit's automakers. Converted auto factories produced millions of engines for airplanes along with other aircraft parts. The Packard Motor Company made Rolls Royce engines for the British Royal Air Force (RAF). Chrysler made bomber fuselages (aircraft bodies). General Motors assembled fighter planes and made wings, landing gears, and other parts for bombers.

President Roosevelt's goals for aircraft production required a huge effort from the aircraft industry as well. In the thirty-two years since the Wright brothers flew the first airplane, America's airplane industry had only made 75,000 aircraft—

most of them by hand. Roosevelt was calling for 60,000 planes in 1942 alone and 125,000 more in 1943. Within two weeks of Pearl Harbor, $6 billion worth of aircraft were on order.

The aircraft industry set about expanding its production at once. Boeing Airplane Company expanded in Seattle. Douglas Aircraft enlarged facilities in Southern California, including a $12-million plant at Long Beach. Bell Aircraft put up a new factory at Niagara Falls, New York, and built a huge bomber factory at Marietta, Georgia. The total number of plane factories increased from forty-one to eighty-one by 1943. Floor space to assemble the craft expanded from 14 million to 170 million square feet.

This expansion was a bonanza for workers. Employment in the aircraft industry rose from 100,000 workers in 1940 to over 2 million by 1945. Although Roosevelt's goals proved unattainable, the factories built 23,000 airplanes a year before Pearl Harbor, 85,898 in 1943, and 96,318 in 1944.

Not only were Americans producing astounding numbers of airplanes, they were also improving aircraft quality. The speed of the B-17 Flying Fortress increased from 256 to 287 miles per hour, and its range was extended from 1,377 miles to 2,000. By the war's end, the B-17 was superseded by the B-29 Superfortress, which was twice as big and could travel one-third farther, carrying two and a half times more bombs.

B-29 Superfortresses drop their bombs on Japan. The aircraft was a major improvement over the B-17.

Before the Germans and Japanese surrendered in 1945, Americans produced 296,429 airplanes, including fighters, scout bombers, torpedo bombers, patrol bombers, amphibians, long-range navy "liberator" bombers, transport- and trainer-type aircraft, and gliders. There were also 200 lighter-than-air nonrigid dirigibles, barrage balloons, and training blimps.

American industry also produced 71,063 naval ships, 5,400 merchant marine ships, and 64,000 landing craft. Submarines were built in the Midwest and launched down the Mississippi River. Shipyards worked twenty-four hours a day to produce mighty battleships, aircraft carriers, cruisers, destroyers, mine layers, patrol and torpedo boats, supply ships, tenders, and oilers.

In addition, industry made 102,351 tanks and self-propelled guns (a trainload of tanks every day); 372,431 artillery pieces; 47 million tons of artillery ammunition; 15 million rifles, machine guns, and pistols; and 44 billion rounds of small-arms ammunition for a total cost of $183 billion. So impressive was this feat that in 1943 Soviet premier Joseph Stalin grudgingly proposed a toast to "American war production, without which this war would have been lost."[25]

The people who owned defense-related businesses were patriotic, but they also made incredible profits from war production. The Walter Kidde Company—producers of fire extinguishers—saw sales lift from $2 million in 1938 to $60 million in 1943, while the number of employees grew from 450 to 5,000. D. W. Onan and Sons—makers of generators—saw sales increase from $300,000 to $50 million and its payroll grow from 60 to 2,100 employees. Hundreds of other war-production factories showed similar astounding increases.

The liberty ship Abraham Lincoln *is launched. Safe from attack, American industry was able to produce large numbers of planes, ships, and artillery.*

Sir Launchalot

The men who oversaw wartime industries sometimes became national heroes. They were masters of industrial mass production and finance who could cut through government red tape and produce needed goods quickly. One such man was shipbuilder Henry J. Kaiser. During the war, Kaiser—a landlubber who had never been in a shipyard before 1942—opened seven shipyards and revolutionized shipbuilding.

Because it took hundreds of skilled craftsmen more than a month to build a ship by tra-

Henry J. Kaiser peers into a furnace used to produce steel at one of his shipbuilding plants.

ditional methods, Kaiser simplified ship construction so that it could be done by less-experienced workers on assembly lines. Traditional shipbuilders laughed at Kaiser's assembly-plant shipyards. They also laughed when he spoke of the "front" and "back" of a ship instead of using the sailor terms "fore, and "aft". But Kaiser's methods were so efficient that he astounded the world by building and launching each ship in only eighty hours.

Kaiser, called "Sir Launchalot," slept only four hours a night. He rushed around the country hiring workers, organizing projects, and busting through government regulations to get steel and other materials. When his shipyards ran short of steel, he borrowed $106 million and built California's first steel mill near Fontana. When he could not obtain raw materials for his mill, he prospected for ore in Utah. In the four years of the war, Kaiser's company manufactured 2,716 liberty ships— merchant vessels that bore the brunt of carrying supplies to the fighting fronts. His ships accounted for a full 27 percent of the total ship tonnage turned out during the war.

Building an Atom Bomb

The most enduring legacy of the war was the development of nuclear weapons. The explosion that shook the world in 1945 was the collective work of thousands of people. It represented an unprecedented collaboration of the military, industry, and science.

Physicists had been trying to crack the code of nuclear power for more than a decade. In 1934 Italian scientist Enrico Fermi proved that the uranium atom could be split. By 1939 more than one hundred academic papers had been published on the subject. This work did not go unnoticed by the Germans. They banned the export of uranium from Czechoslovakia—a country with one of the world's few known deposits of the element.

By this time Fermi had immigrated to the United States. He tried to warn the government about the danger of Germany developing an atom bomb, but his warnings went unheeded. He turned to fellow physicist Albert Einstein, who sent a letter to Roosevelt warning that the Germans might build a bomb that "carried by a boat or exploded in a port, might well destroy the whole port together with the surrounding territory."[26] (Since Einstein's theories allowed others to build atomic weapons, he later regretted his involvement with the bomb.)

Roosevelt formed a committee to pursue building the bomb. After the attack on Pearl Harbor, research, under the code name Manhattan Project, began in earnest. Scientists who worked on the top-secret project endured censored mail and tapped telephones. They were trailed by bodyguards and forbidden from opening checking accounts lest their identities be revealed. The Manhattan Project was so secretive that, when Roosevelt died, Vice President Truman did not even know of its existence. He was told the next day.

The building of an atomic bomb cost more than $2 billion and was dispersed through twelve hundred contracts assigned to twenty-five universities and thirty-seven industrial enterprises. The project involved more than 120,000 people in nineteen states and Canada. Three weeks after the first nuclear explosion in New Mexico, the bomb was dropped on Japan.

Wartime Prosperity

The sheer volume of war contracts ensured full employment and prosperity for

Enrico Fermi (top) and Albert Einstein warned President Roosevelt that Germany may have been developing an atomic weapon.

millions of Americans who had just suffered through twelve years of the Great Depression. In spite of wartime restrictions, many Americans were finally able to buy many necessities as well as comfort items that they had been dreaming about for years. Business and farm profits were rising along with wages and salaries. At every level of society, men, women, and even children had money to spend for luxuries. During the war 17 million new jobs were created and the index of industrial production nearly doubled.

Average incomes also nearly doubled. The average yearly income in New York in 1938 was $2,760. By 1943 it had jumped to $4,044. In Los Angeles it went from $2,031 to $3,469. In Washington, D.C., the relative income climbed from $2,227 to $5,316. Overall, personal income soared from $96 billion before the war to $171 billion during the war years.

New job opportunities and prosperity reached all levels of American society. Farmers, businesspeople, women, African Americans, skilled workers, unskilled workers, and others shared in the good times. The biggest gains came to poor people whose incomes rose an average of 68 percent. Gains also came to the tax collectors. In 1940 only 7.8 million people filed income tax returns. In 1945—because of the new withholding tax—over 48 million people filed.

The war also had an effect on the wealthy. Food rationing and shortages fell on the rich and poor alike. And many

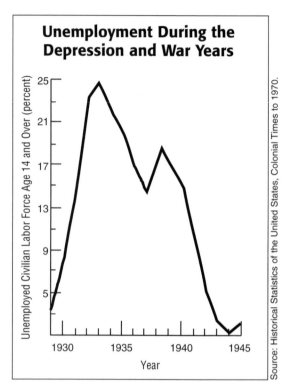

Unemployment During the Depression and War Years

Unemployed Civilian Labor Force Age 14 and Over (percent)

Year

Source: Historical Statistics of the United States, Colonial Times to 1970.

rich people permanently lost servants to high-paying factory jobs. By 1944 the number of women doing domestic work fell by 20 percent.

Even teenagers were getting ahead. The war's growing appetite for able-bodied workers opened up thousands of good-paying jobs to teenage boys and girls. Many states relaxed child labor laws for the duration of the war, and by 1943 over 3 million American boys and girls were working in fields and factories. Over five hundred thousand teens worked at defense plants where they were paid the same as the older workers. Lockheed Aircraft alone hired fifteen hundred boys as draftsmen, riveters, electricians, and sheet-metal workers. The teens proved themselves worthy of their pay, but many dropped out of school or fell asleep in class, weary from the demands of their jobs.

Disabled workers were also in great demand because of the labor shortage. A commission before the war showed only 27,703 disabled people in the workforce. In 1943 that number jumped to nearly 200,000. The disabled performed many jobs. Blind workers, for instance, sorted sweepings in airplane plants to salvage rivets that were dropped; they were able to distinguish by touch eight different rivets used.

Nation on the Move

Because of all the new jobs offered at the defense plants, America was a nation on the move during the war. More than 31 million people left home, 15.3 million to find jobs and 16 million to serve in the armed forces. According to the census bureau, almost 8 million Americans moved across state lines, and 4 million moved to different parts of the country. Over 1.4 million moved to California to work in the shipyards and aircraft plants located there.

As a result of the massive population shift, acute housing shortages developed. In boomtowns such as San Diego, San Francisco, Seattle, Baton Rouge, Los Angeles, Philadelphia, Detroit, and Portland, Oregon, the sheer numbers of people overwhelmed existing housing, schools, and other public facilities. In-

stant slums consisting of shantytowns, trailer parks, villages, and tent settlements grew up around many cities. But as American author John Dos Passos, wrote: "Housekeeping in a trailer with electric lights and running water is a dazzling luxury to a woman who's lived all her life in a cabin with half-inch chinks between the splintered boards in the floor." [27]

The boomtown experience was even greater in the South—a region that had been economically depressed ever since the Civil War ended in 1865. The resurgence stemmed mostly from the scores of military training camps being built there. One example of this drastic change was Stark, Florida, a town of fifteen hundred people in 1940. When it was determined that Camp Blanding would be located there, twenty thousand men were employed to build the facility. Local hotels were filled, and citizens opened their homes to those in need. Those who could not find housing lived in cars, lean-tos, brush piles, and even packing crates. When the camp opened, sixty thousand soldiers quickly arrived, making Stark the fourth largest city in Florida at the time.

Along the Gulf Coast, shipyards drew tens of thousands of job seekers from backwoods farms. The population of Mobile, Alabama, shot up 60 percent in three years. The area was so crowded that landlords rented twenty-five-cent "hot beds" to workers who would rent the bed to sleep for eight hours.

The most notorious slum was near the

Wartime Train Travel

During the war years nearly every train station, bus depot, and airport was filled to capacity with military personnel and workers on the move. The railroads carried 97 percent of the traffic, moving more than a million military personnel a month and a total of 43.7 million by the war's end.

Materials to maintain the rolling stock were in short supply, along with skilled workers to perform the tasks. Like many other American resources, the railroads were used well beyond their capacity. Although most rail lines were converting to diesel power, every locomotive, whether steam or electric, was pressed into service.

Although the government urged civilians to stay home, the lure of jobs in faraway cities was too great to resist. Railways logged triple the passenger miles traveled between 1941 and 1944. In 1942 alone, American trains tallied 55 billion passenger miles.

Troop movement required half of all available Pullman (sleeping) cars. Civilians were packed onto cramped coach seats at night. Since troop trains had track priority, they often forced civilian trains to remain idle on railroad sidings for hours on end while dozens of troop trains chugged past.

The military had first call on all reservations, and civilians were treated to cattle-car conditions; however, many passengers were grateful even for standing room.

The men and women who ran America's railroads, whether from an office, a station, or on the train, worked long hours in all kinds of weather so that troops, civilians, and war goods could reach their destinations.

Willow Run plant. The aircraft plant attracted thirty-two thousand new residents to the area, and the shiny new factory contrasted cruelly with the primitive living conditions around it. A typical house in the area had five men living in the basement, a family of five on the first floor, four people on the second floor, nine men living in the garage, and four trailers housing four families in the backyard. Toilets consisted of outhouses perched dangerously close to water wells.

Women in the Workforce

With millions of men fighting overseas, America looked to its women to bring the workforce up to strength. Women in the workforce faced ingrained prejudice. (In the prewar world, unlike today, factory, industrial, and other blue-collar jobs were only held by men.)

It took the government to persuade industrial bosses that women could work as well as men. To do this, an advertising campaign was instituted. Billboards showed women asking, "What job is mine on the Victory line?" and supplied some ready answers: "If you followed recipes exactly for making cakes, you can learn to load a shell."[28] The campaign worked. Five million women joined the defense industry.

Women workers were called "Soldiers Without Guns," "Dames for Defense," "Winnie the Welder," or "Rosie the Riveter." (The real Rosie the Riveter was an airplane factory worker named Rosina Bonavita.)

Women quickly proved that they

could perform any job. Women went to work driving streamrollers, semis, garbage trucks, and taxis. In the Pacific Northwest, four thousand women logged the hillsides—they were called "lumberjills" instead of lumberjacks. Women learned to rivet, weld, and operate giant cranes in war industries. Soon they were doing everything from cutting tool dies to loading shells to assembling airplane fuse-

Two women help assemble a fighter plane. Many women took jobs that were left open when men joined the military.

lages. Women worked as aircraft mechanics as well as punch- and drill-press operators. They also learned to holler and curse right alongside their tough, middle-aged male coworkers. There was only one major difference between women workers and men: Women were paid less, even less than the teenage boys with whom they worked.

Women had to adopt their dress and habits to factory environments. On the job, women had to wear practical clothing. Some companies hired leading designers to create stylish work uniforms, but most simply required sturdy shoes and pants or jumpsuits. Long hair posed another—possibly deadly—problem if caught in machinery. Working women solved this problem by tying their hair in turbans, bandannas, kerchiefs, or net hoods. Many wore steel hard hats.

The biggest problem faced by working women was shopping and caring for children. Department and grocery stores stayed open late to meet the needs of working women, but day care was in short supply. After great debate, the government built twenty-eight hundred day-care centers, but this was only sufficient for 10 percent of the children of working mothers.

Of the millions of women who joined the workforce, a greater number were unpaid volunteers. No one was too old or too young to perform vital services during the war. In Tennessee, two-thousand teenage girls harvested 1 million gallons of strawberries. In New England, women in their seventies took turns at round-the-clock plane spotting. More than 3 million women joined the Red Cross to run canteens, serve as nurses' aides, or drive ambulances. More than 1 million others provided food, entertainment, company, and good cheer for lonely servicemen at United Service Organization for National Defense centers (USOs) across the nation.

Although 80 percent of women workers voiced a desire to keep their job after the war, industry was eager to hire returning male veterans. This quickly forced women out of their jobs once the war ended. By the spring of 1944 large companies began running ads such as the one showing a crying child. The text read: "Mother, when will you stay home again?" The ad then went on to say, "Some jubilant day mother will stay home again, doing the job she likes best—making a home for you and daddy, when he gets back."[29]

Chapter 5

Racial Hostility Against Americans

As the devastation of the Pearl Harbor attack sank in, virulent hatred of all things Japanese emerged. Store owners took hammers to any items marked Made in Japan and stacked the broken pieces in store windows. In Washington, D.C., angry men chopped down four of the three thousand cherry trees that the citizens of Tokyo had presented to America in 1912. In Nashville, Tennessee, the Department of Conservation requested 6 million hunting licenses to hunt Japanese invaders at a fee of two dollars apiece.

The term *enemy aliens* was used to describe everyone of Japanese, German, and Italian descent—this included about 1 million people in a country of 132 million. Within weeks of the declaration of war, many people in these racial groups fell under the investigation of the FBI, military intelligence, and even local police forces.

Prior to the war, several thousand German Americans belonged to the Bund, a Nazi front group that staged loud rallies

---

A woman points to a sign that declares that Japanese are not welcomed in her town. Such racism was inflamed by the attack on Pearl Harbor.

Crisis in Little Tokyo

About 150,000 people of Japanese descent were living on the west coast at the start of the war. The greatest concentration of Japanese Americans was in the Los Angeles neighborhood still known as Little Tokyo. On the day after the Pearl Harbor bombing, the Associated Press reported the reaction of people in Little Tokyo. The story was reprinted in the book *World War II, 1939–1945*.

> Almost everyone in Little Tokyo, the largest Japanese settlement in the United States, expected war between Japan and America.
>
> None expressed the view that Japan can win. Most believe that the military government of Nippon is committing national hara-kiri (suicide).
>
> Little Tokyo, near Los Angeles' towering City Hall is the home of 40,000 members of the Japanese race. Twenty thousand more, out of the Pacific Coast's total of 150,000 resided elsewhere in Los Angeles County.
>
> Two-thirds of those are Japanese only in an ethnological sense. They are the Nisei, or second-generation, American-born. Their parents, the first generation, are denied citizenship but have lived here 20, 30 or more years.
>
> "This is an unprecedented crisis for us," says Katsuma Mukseda, president of the Japanese Cultural Society, "but we shall acquit ourselves proudly. America is our home, our permanent residence."
>
> Togo Tanaka, editor of [a Japanese-American newspaper] pointed out that the Japanese-American Citizens League . . . has been working closely with the F.B.I. and naval intelligence for several years.
>
> "We think the Japanese government is stupid and has embarked on a campaign it has absolutely no chance of winning," said Tanaka. . . . "This may be the end of Japan as a power."

In spite of their pledge of allegiance to the United States, Japanese-American schoolchildren were considered a threat to U.S. security.

and showed propaganda films. The activities of the Bund were mostly confined to neighborhoods with a strong German background, such as the Yorkville section of Manhattan and the German quarter in St. Louis.

Many Italian Americans took pride in the accomplishments of Mussolini's Italy. And prior to the war, most Italian-American newspapers were pro-Fascist. Roosevelt summed up the widely held attitude when he told his attorney general, "I don't care so much about the Italians, they are a lot of opera singers, but the Germans are different. They may be dangerous."[30] After war was declared, five thousand German Americans and Italian Americans were rounded up and interned at Ellis Island in New York. Within a year they were released.

The main hatred was focused on Japanese Americans. Because of their Asian features, they were easier to identify than Germans or Italians. People automatically equated them with the pilots who had bombed Pearl Harbor. Two-thirds of America's 150,000 Japanese Americans were native-born U.S. citizens, but this did not stop the suspicion and hostility directed toward them.

Prejudice Against Japanese Americans

Most of the Japanese Americans in the United States lived in California, Oregon, and Washington. With the Pacific Fleet crippled, people on the west coast felt particularly vulnerable to a Japanese attack. In this atmosphere, the anti-Asian prejudice that had plagued the west coast for more than one hundred years reached crisis proportions. The ugly mood was summed up by Lieutenant General John DeWitt, who was in charge of the west coast's defense: "A Jap's a Jap! It

makes no difference whether he's an American or not."[31]

Japanese store owners put huge signs on their establishments that read I Am An American. Despite their efforts, banks still refused to cash their checks, insurance companies canceled their policies, and milkmen and grocers refused to deliver or sell them anything.

Pressure to retaliate against Japanese Americans mounted. This led Roosevelt to sign Executive Order 9066 on February 19, 1942, authorizing the secretary of the war to designate certain areas of the country as "military areas" and to exile all persons from them. Although cloaked in broad language, this order was aimed directly at Japanese Americans. In the

His sign posted in vain, this Japanese-American businessman lost his store and would soon be relocated to an internment camp.

spring and summer of 1942, over 112,000 Japanese Americans were moved to temporary camps.

DeWitt's soldiers immediately began rounding up Japanese Americans. Most were given as little as forty-eight hours' notice to dispose of their businesses, farms, and homes. They quickly fell prey to bargain hunters who acquired their belongings for a fraction of their true value.

The displaced Americans dragged off bedrolls, baggage, and their frightened children to hastily converted assembly centers. These temporary camps were often racetracks or fairgrounds where many people were forced to bed down in horse stalls still reeking of manure. Most of the Japanese Americans went without a fight, hoping to prove their loyalty to a country that had turned on them.

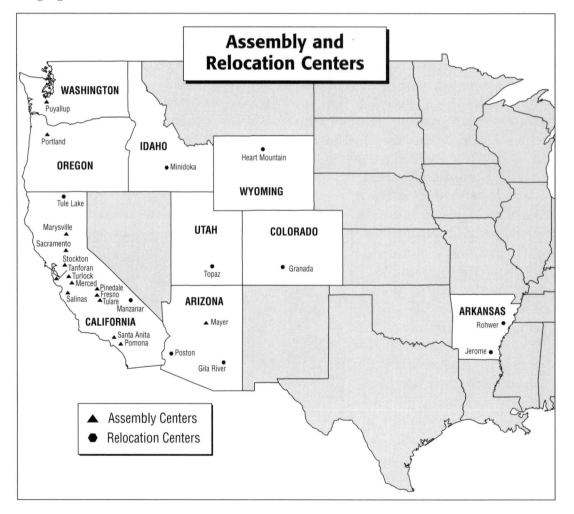

Assembly and Relocation Centers

WASHINGTON
Puyallup

Portland

OREGON

IDAHO

Minidoka

Heart Mountain

WYOMING

Tule Lake

Marysville

Sacramento

Stockton
Tanforan
Turlock
Merced
Pinedale
Fresno
Salinas
Tulare
Manzanar

CALIFORNIA

Santa Anita
Pomona

UTAH

Topaz

COLORADO

Granada

ARIZONA

Mayer

Poston

Gila River

ARKANSAS
Rohwer

Jerome

▲ Assembly Centers
⬢ Relocation Centers

The prisoners were eventually shipped farther inland to ten permanent camps in barren and isolated areas of six western states and Arkansas. Even Roosevelt referred to these with the ugly term *concentration camps.* Some of the camps, like the Heart Mountain Relocation Center in Wyoming experienced winter temperatures of thirty degrees below zero.

Each camp held about ten thousand persons, and every family was assigned a twenty-by-twenty-five-foot apartment, often made of tar paper over wooden planks. The apartments contained potbellied stoves and shelves and furniture made from scrap lumber.

The Japanese Americans attempted to maintain their dignity at the camps. The illusion of a stable, small-town existence was enforced by the operations of complete fire, police, and post office departments. There were schools, hospitals, camp newspapers, and even entertainment. In most camps internees were put to work making camouflage netting and other military necessities.

After a year or two, some of the prisoners had their rights restored to them and were allowed to settle in areas outside the west coast. Young people were eager to get out, but many old people, their lives now shattered, did not want to leave the camps. They felt they could not start over in the twilight of their lives.

A Japanese family awaits the arrival of a government bus to take them to a relocation camp. The children wear ID tags in case they are separated from their parents.

During the course of the war, ten people were charged with spying for Japan—all of them were Caucasian. Not a single Japanese American was ever charged with espionage, sabotage, or treason. In fact, like every other American, the internees were subject to the draft. "The biggest irony of all," one internee later recalled, "was seeing my three older brothers being drafted, one by one, out of our camp."[32]

Over eight thousand Japanese Americans served in the U.S. armed forces, many with great distinction in combat.

Navajo Code Talkers

American missions against Japan were severely compromised because the Japanese were breaking American codes just as fast as they could be devised. The only form of radio communication that was secure were those spoken by Navajo Indians, speaking in a coded form of their own language—a code the Japanese never broke.

In late 1941 the marines recruited hundreds of Navajo men from reservations in Arizona and New Mexico to relay vital communications between units in the Pacific. The Navajo code talkers took part in every assault the marines conducted in the Pacific between 1942 and 1945.

The idea to use the Navajo language for secure communications came from Philip Johnson, who was one of the few non-Navajo who could speak the language fluently. Johnson believed that Navajo would meet military requirements because it is an unwritten language of extreme complexity. In the 1940s less than thirty non-Navajo individuals could understand the language.

The marines found that the Navajo could encode, transmit, and decode a three-line English message in twenty seconds. A decoding machine took thirty minutes to perform the same task. In May 1942 the first twenty-nine Navajo recruits created and memorized the code.

The code talkers transmitted information on tactics and troop movement and relayed orders and other vital battlefield communications over telephones and radios. During the battle of Iwo Jima, six Navajo code talkers worked around the clock during the first two days of fighting. Those six sent and received over eight hundred messages, all without error.

Long unrecognized because of the continued value of their language as a classified security code, the Navajo code talkers of World War II were honored for their contributions to defense on September 17, 1992, at the Pentagon in Washington, D.C.

Two Navajo code talkers help send vital messages between units in the jungles of the Pacific.

During their exile, the Japanese Americans lost nearly half a billion dollars in assets, of which only about 10 percent was ever returned to them by the government. In 1988 the U.S. government issued a formal apology to the Japanese Americans who were confined against their will during World War II.

African Americans in the Military

While the Japanese were relative newcomers to America, African Americans had been living in the United States for centuries. But 1 million blacks who entered the military service found a system of discrimination more rigid than the one they faced in civilian life. For most of the war a policy of strict racial segregation prevailed in the military. In training camps, blacks were forced into separate dining and recreational facilities. Army units were segregated by race, and no black officer could outrank a white one.

At the beginning of the war, the navy only accepted blacks as mess (dining hall) attendants. The marines would not recruit any blacks. Official government policy, approved by Roosevelt in 1940,

stated that integration would "produce situations destructive to morale and detrimental to the preparation for national defense."[33] The army and the Red Cross went even farther. The Red Cross separated blood plasma donated by blacks and whites, even though the man who had perfected the method for preserving the plasma—Dr. Charles R. Drew—was himself an African American.

Nothing was more absurd than the case of privileges extended to German

---

Black recruits line up for training exercises in Illinois in 1943. Strict racial segregation was enforced in all branches of the military.

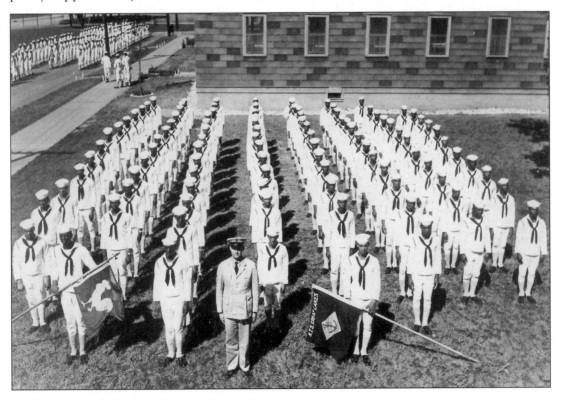

prisoners of war (POWs) in the United States. In Salina, Kansas, German POWs were allowed to leave their prison camp and dine in restaurants on Main Street. When the black soldiers who guarded them tried to enter the restaurant, the counterman said, "You know we don't serve colored here."[34]

Soldier Lloyd Brown and several other black servicemen were guarding the Germans. Brown later reflected:

> We ignored [the counterman] and just stood there inside the door, staring at what we had come to see—the German prisoners of war having lunch at the counter. If we were . . . in Germany they would break our bones. As "colored" men in Salina, they only break our hearts.[35]

The struggle for equal rights was intensified when African Americans stationed in Europe found they were treated better by the local people than by their own countrymen. In Britain, when fights broke out between white and black GIs, British bystanders would often join in on the side of the blacks. After one such clash in Leicester, signs appeared on bars and restaurants stating, "For British Civilians and U.S.A. Negro Forces Only."[36]

Blacks in Civilian Life

The upheavals caused by World War II also deeply affected the 13 million African Americans who were not in the military. For blacks, the war years marked an agonizing period in the struggle for equal rights.

Defense industries and trade unions practiced rigid segregation. It was so blatant that during the prewar defense buildup one aircraft company employed only ten blacks among its workforce of thirty thousand. At the Kinsbury Ordnance Plant in Indiana—which was completely constructed with federal funds—there was a special production line for blacks, separate toilets, and even a bomb shelter marked "For Colored Only."

A black college student quoted in *The Home Front, U.S.A.*, summed up the prevailing attitudes of African Americans:

> The Army jim crows (segregates) us. The Navy lets us serve only as messmen. The Red Cross refuses our blood. Employers and labor unions shut us out. Lynchings continue. We are disenfranchised, jim crowed and spat upon. What more could Hitler do than that?[37]

Some blacks expressed sympathy for the Japanese. A poll of African Americans in New York City showed that 18 percent believed they would be treated better under Japanese rule than in white America. Elijah Muhammad, leader of the Black Muslims, was even arrested for his pro-Japanese sympathies. He served four years in prison for sedition and draft evasion.

Most black leaders, however, urged full support of the war effort. They felt that they would be rewarded with equal rights if they worked as equals in defense factories and in the military. The first major move toward that goal came in 1941. When African American leaders threatened a massive equal rights march on Washington, Roosevelt signed Executive Order 8802, which forbade racial discrimination in the defense industries, an order that was seldom enforced.

The threatened march on Washington signaled a new turn in the civil rights struggle. Black leaders focused on the hypocrisy of a nation waging a war on fascism abroad while maintaining segregation in the service and at home. Aroused by this notion, membership in the National Association for the Advancement of Colored People (NAACP) increased ninefold. Other groups such as the Congress of Racial Equality (CORE) formed in the South and adopted nonviolent tactics of civil disobedience.

But times remained hard for African Americans during the war years. While black employment rose by 1 million and the number of skilled workers doubled, the average black family's income by the end of the war was still only half that of the average white family's.

Race Riots

The racism practiced against African Americans fueled their impatience and discontent. In 1943 this fueled riots in several American cities—Springfield, Massachusetts; El Paso and Port Arthur, Texas; Hubbard, Ohio; and Harlem in

Black women welders at work at the Kaiser Shipyards in Richmond, California. Defense contractors separated their employees according to race.

New York City. The worst race riot occurred in Detroit.

Northern cities near defense plants, such as Detroit, Pittsburgh, and Cleveland, were inundated with black workers from the South. Detroit saw sixty thousand new black immigrants who were forced to live in the squalor of the misnamed Paradise Valley, a sixty-block slum where sewage ran through the streets. The neighborhood was bad, but the factory workers were earning decent pay for the first time.

Blacks were not the only southerners who had moved to Detroit. Many white people from the South also came for the defense jobs—and they brought their prejudices with them. White workers regarded the new prosperity of blacks as a threat to their own status. Whites, too, were living in overcrowded neighborhoods.

On a humid afternoon in June 1943, racial fistfights broke out in a crowded park on Belle Isle on the Detroit River. Rumors spread that a black man had raped and killed a white woman. Black people said that whites had killed a black woman and her baby. Soon a full-scale race riot exploded.

Blacks from Paradise Valley looted and burned white-owned stores. White mobs fought back, shooting black people at random. Before federal troops broke up the riot thirty-six hours later, nine whites and twenty-five blacks were dead. Seventeen of the blacks had been killed by police.

Zoot Suit Riot

Teenage rebels during World War II sometimes wore zoot suits—long coats that reached the knees and had padded shoulders. The coat was worn unbuttoned to reveal baggy pants that tapered from sixteen inches wide at the knee to six inches at the cuff. The ensemble was highlighted by a long key chain that almost dragged on the floor and topped off by a broad-brimmed felt hat. Zoot suiters sometimes carried switchblade knives while their girlfriends carried whiskey flasks that were shaped to fit inside their bras.

The zoot suit originated in Harlem—the African-American neighborhood in New York City. The style quickly spread to other urban areas and became a widespread fad among teens. To some, the zoot suit simply represented an outrageous costume teens wore before they would be forced to wear drab military garb. To others, it was the uniform of street gangs, an affront to established order, and a symbol of rebellion and lawlessness.

In Los Angeles, the zoot suit was a favorite among Mexican-American teens. In 1942 a series of small clashes between zoot suiters and GIs caused the law to crack down on zoot suiters.

The hatred reached a climax in June 1943 when rumor spread that a sailor had been beaten up by a gang of zoot suiters. A mob of twenty-five hundred soldiers and sailors gathered, vowing to wage a cleanup campaign. They began pummeling about one hundred young Mexican Americans and ripping off their zoot suits. The Los Angeles city council reacted to the zoot suit riot by making it against the law to wear a zoot suit.

Two zoot suiters, one beaten and the other stripped, try to recover after being attacked by American servicemen in Los Angeles.

The riots did have a positive effect on the country, however. They highlighted the race problem to average Americans. Before the riots 62 percent of whites thought black people were happy with the way things were in America. After the riots that number fell to 25 percent. Over two hundred cities and towns set up interracial committees to study the problem.

The seeds of change were also sown in the military. In 1944 the army ordered desegregation of its training facilities, but the change was slow, especially in the South. When a manpower shortage occurred during the Battle of the Bulge, the army attached black platoons to white companies. But integration did not go beyond that. It was not until after the war—July 26, 1948—that President Truman signed the order to desegregate the armed forces.

Jewish People in America

One of Adolf Hitler's sworn missions was to murder every Jewish man, woman, and child in Europe. To this end, the Nazis exterminated over 6 million Jewish citizens during the war.

In America, Jewish people did not face discrimination at the levels directed towards African Americans and Japanese Americans. But polls showed that Americans distrusted Jews more than any other European people except Italians.

At the time of the war, many Jews in the United States were poor recent immigrants. Application forms for working in the defense industry questioned the applicant about his or her religion. Those who said they were Jewish were usually not hired. About 30 percent of the want ads in the *New York Times* and *Herald Tribune* expressed a preference for Protestants or Catholics.

Anti-Semitism—hatred against Jews—was stirred up in America by a popular radio host named Father Charles E. Coughlin. His radio show, which reached over 1 million people, preached hatred against Jews and blacks. Although he was taken off the air by the government for his hate-filled propaganda, Coughlin continued to publish a

Radio host Father Charles E. Coughlin fueled hatred against Jews and blacks with his anti-Semitic, racist speeches and magazine.

magazine called *Social Justice*, which reached two hundred thousand people. In a typical article, he wrote: "The Jew should retire from the field of politics and government. He has no more business in that sphere than a pig in a china shop."[38] Coughlin also spread the false idea that Jews had started World War II for their own profit and then evaded the draft to let the Christians do the fighting. *Social Justice* was sold in front of Catholic churches after Sunday mass.

The most heart-rending problems for Jewish people were the result of federal immigration policy. The Immigration Act of 1924 severely restricted the number of Jews who could immigrate to America. As the Nazis tightened their grip on Europe, Jews and other threatened people tried to save themselves by fleeing Hitler's domain, but they were denied access to the United States. Spain and Turkey, fearful of Nazi reprisals, provided only limited sanctuary. The British refused to let Jews flee to British-ruled Palestine because Great Britain desperately needed the oil provided by Arab states, which were violently opposed to Jewish immigration.

The demand for immigration visas far outstripped the quotas set by Congress in 1924. And only 8 percent of the American people polled were willing to admit more Jewish refugees from Europe. Although Roosevelt could have issued an executive order to ease the restrictions, he did not.

Roosevelt himself was popular with American Jews, however, and the president employed several high-profile Jewish people in the executive branch. As news of Nazi atrocities at concentration camps drifted back to the States, the House and Senate both passed resolutions for the punishment of war crimes, including genocide against the Jews.

Anti-Semitism eased somewhat in America in 1945 when movies of concentration camps shown in national theaters. The horrors on the screen showed many people for the first time what anti-Semitism, carried to extremes, meant.

The war only magnified racial attitudes that were already rampant in America. But it also exposed the evil behind these attitudes. Because of the prejudice exhibited against minorities during the war—especially Japanese Americans—racial attitudes began to change. By the 1950s millions of white people would support African Americans and others in

Chapter 6

News and Entertainment

The pressures and tensions brought on by the war—along with a booming economy—drove people to spend lavishly on entertainment. Wartime business in nightclubs was up 40 percent. Betting and racetrack attendance reached their all-time highest levels during the war. Broadway enjoyed its most prosperous theater season in 1944–1945. The movie business was also booming. Theaters stayed open practically all night to accommodate swing-shift factory workers who worked from 4:00 P.M. to 1:00 A.M. (The term *swing shift* was coined by workers who labored at night. They imagined that the day-shift workers were out at clubs dancing, having a ball, and "swinging it" at night.)

As in other industries, government propaganda popped up in all aspects of entertainment from magazines and newspapers to movies. Women's magazines were full of wartime fashions, jukeboxes played war songs, and plays and Hollywood movies had military and patriotic themes. Even Mickey Mouse and Donald Duck were put to work fighting Hitler's war machine. The government worked twenty-four hours a day restricting and coordinating what Americans heard and read.

Censorship and War Information

Americans had to accept limits on freedom of expression during the war era. The agency in charge of limiting information was the Office of Censorship. Oftentimes Americans would receive letters from loved ones overseas only to find that they had been slit open, a few words or sentences were snipped out, and the envelopes were resealed and marked "Opened by Censor."

The head of the Office of Censorship was respected newsman Byron Price. Price also instituted a voluntary code for publishers and broadcasters. News of ship and troop movements and battle casualties was severely restricted.

The manipulation of symbols and words—propaganda—was the main function of the Office of War Information (OWI). It was established in 1942 with the mandate to

coordinate the dissemination of war information by all federal agencies and to formulate and carry out, by means of the press, radio, and motion pictures, programs designed to facilitate an understanding . . . of the war effort . . . and policies of the government.[39]

This mandate implied much more than the broadcasting of facts and figures. It also had to explain and defend government policies and keep certain information from becoming public.

The OWI decided which government shows to put on the air and ranked them in importance. Advertisers and stations were also supplied with fact sheets from which the producers could develop their own pro-government messages.

At the request of the OWI, radio stations nationwide agreed to give a certain amount of time each week to war programs. The plans were worked out so that the entertainment portions of many leading radio shows were built around wartime messages. For in-

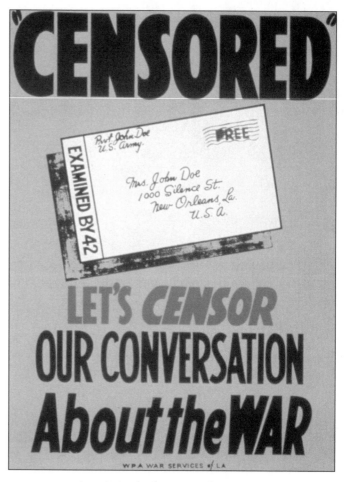

Americans had to accept a certain amount of censorship during the war. This poster asks the public to not talk about the war in private correspondence.

stance, an entire thirty-minute-long radio drama might be about food conservation or rationing. Children's shows dramatized the favorite recycling program among kids—tin and paper salvage.

The OWI also knew that Hollywood could serve a major part in the war propaganda effort. In 1941 the president himself addressed the thirteenth annual Academy Awards, via radio, and reminded the film industry that it was responsible for solidifying the nation's resolve in support of a strong national defense. By that time movies were the sixth largest industry in the United States; and, throughout the war, Hollywood films were monitored by the OWI.

Award-Winning Reporters

President Roosevelt set up another agency to give information to the working press—the Office of Facts and Figures (OFF). Its mission was to give "factual information on the defense effort and to facilitate a widespread understanding of the status and progress of that effort."[40] To accomplish this, OFF furnished hard data to the press and radio. OFF also had to control information so as not to reveal details about defense production or military maneuvers.

These conditions irritated members of the working press, who resented the establishment of one central clearinghouse for information. This resentment was widespread in vital news stories such as the one about Pearl Harbor; casualty figures and exact details of the attack were kept under wraps for over a year.

Later in the war, the press rose to occasions of award-winning reporting. The most widely read and loved war correspondent was Ernie Pyle. He did not depict soldiers as rigid military men but as regular guys—civilians in uniform. Pyle covered the war for the Scripps-Howard papers, beginning with the invasion of North Africa. His columns eventually appeared six days a week in 310 papers with more than 12 million readers.

Pyle concentrated on the dirty details of a soldier's life and death—for example, the debris of shoes, cigarettes, and writing paper left behind by the dead on Normandy beach. Pyle's writing style is demonstrated in the following excerpt

This bust of journalist Ernie Pyle resides in the National Portrait Gallery. Pyle was known for his gritty writing style that allowed Americans to view the war from the GI's point of view.

about a company commander who had been killed in the hills of Italy. The men in the company slowly passed by the commander's body, which lay on the side of the road.

> [A soldier] squatted down, and he reached and took the Captain's hand, and he sat there for a full five minutes holding the dead hand in his own and looking intently into the dead face. And he never uttered a sound all the time he sat there.
>
> Finally he put the hand down. He reached up and gently straightened the points of the Captain's shirt collar, and then sort of rearranged the tattered edges of his uniform around the wound, and then he got up and walked away down the road in the moonlight.[41]

Pyle's illustrious writing career ended when he was killed in a foxhole during the battle of Iwo Jima in 1945.

Comic Strips

Americans longed to escape from their problems, and comic strips helped sell as many papers as war stories. The daily comic pages had a total readership of 70 million during the war years. The ten most popular strips were *Joe Palooka, Blondie, Lil' Abner, Little Orphan Annie, Terry and the Pirates, Dick Tracy, Moon Mullins, Gasoline Alley, Bringing Up Father,* and *The Gumps.* The war era witnessed a few battle-oriented comics, notably Bill Maudlin's Pulitzer Prize–winning *Up Front,* which featured a couple of GIs named Willie and Joe.

Several comic heroes—and heroines—joined the military. Joe Palooka and Snuffy Smith joined the army, Barney Google was in the navy, and Dick Tracy was in naval intelligence while doubling as a crime fighter at home.

Like modern TV characters, comic strip characters had fanatical followers who would eagerly discuss each storyline with their friends. When Joe Palooka shot a Nazi in the back, thousands of letters poured into newspapers saying that their hero would not shoot anyone in the back—even a Nazi. When the rumor spread that a character called Skeezix was going to be killed in the war, switchboards at New York's *Daily News* and Chicago's *Tribune* were jammed for three days before the rumor was squelched.

Comic books were as popular as newspaper comics. America's favorite superheroes were Captain Marvel, Superman, and Batman and Robin. The caped crusaders fought Hitler, Tojo, Mussolini, and other enemies. Heroes like the Flash, the Green Lantern, and Johnny Thunder joined forces to fight American spies at home.

The Disney studios did their part in morale building. Disney characters appeared on military insignia, patches, emblems, and flags. These items featured Donald Duck and Mickey Mouse wielding machine guns and throwing bombs. Donald also appeared in successful war cartoons such as *Der Fuehrer's Face*, originally called *Donald Duck in Nutziland*. In this cartoon, Donald falls asleep and dreams that he encounters awful German food, Adolf Hitler, and a goose-stepping Nazi ballet. He awakens clutching a miniature Statue of Liberty.

Other cartoon characters who appeared on home-front posters were Bambi, Pinocchio, Goofy, and Pluto.

Radio

Broadcast television did not exist during World War II. But the radio of the 1940s served the same purpose that TV does today—people received the bulk of their entertainment and music from it. In fact, radio was the number one source of news for most Americans. By 1944 NBC alone was devoting 20 percent of its air time to news, compared with 3.6 percent in 1939. Likewise, 30 percent of CBS radio was dedicated to news.

World War II changed the sound and method of live coverage. According to reporter Bryson Rash, quoted in *America Remembers the Home Front,*

It was the war that really developed electronic journalism. Prior to World War II there weren't many people on the air doing news. The capability of conveying war via electronic media occurred in the Spanish civil war, where for the first time you got broadcasts from battlegrounds, from areas of conflict and capitals that were at war. I think one of the most famous of these early broadcasts was H. V. Kaltenborn reporting on the Spanish war with the sound of guns heard in the background. Then we had the electronic capability of instant communications via shortwave, and that was something new.[42]

Radio was the main source of news during the war. This man's son, whose photo sits atop the radio, is serving with the army air force.

The first live reports of the war were broadcast in 1938, when Germany invaded Czechoslovakia. Events were brought live into people's living rooms by reporters on the scene describing the action as it unfolded.

Reporters, whose disembodied voices boomed over the radio waves, became celebrities. Edward R. Murrow—America's most famous reporter—broadcast from London during the blitz. Murrow's vivid impressions of burning buildings in the night were heard over the background noise of bombs exploding, sirens wailing, and the booming chimes on the clock tower known as Big Ben.

Radio's foreign correspondents reported from the front lines of the war. Murrow broadcast from a Flying Fortress over Berlin. Larry Tinge covered the invasion of Okinawa from a B-29 under heavy attack. Richard Hottelet described his experience parachuting from a burning bomber. Eric Sevareid reported about bailing out of a plane and trekking through the jungles of Burma. George Hicks' broadcast from the deck of a ship during the D-day invasion. These transmissions were sent to networks via shortwave radio. Others were recorded on tape recorders and flown to the nearest transmitter to be relayed to networks back in the States.

The average American listened to the radio four and a half hours a day. Some listeners had shortwave radios and could pick up German propaganda or the British Broadcasting Company's coded

American reporter Edward R. Morrow was famous for his live reports from London, including his observations of the terrible bombings during the Blitz.

broadcasts to underground fighters in Europe.

Radio stations beefed up their security so that saboteurs could not commandeer them. Some popular radio programs were banned by the OWI; weather reports were discontinued until 1943 out of fear that Axis bomber pilots could tune in. Man-on-the-street interviews were dropped on the theory that enemy agents might be employed to send coded messages. Musical request shows were banned for the same reason. As one nervous official suggested,

"The 'Star-Spangled Banner' can be played in a manner to convey a message from someone in Kansas City to someone in Mexico."[43]

In February 1943 a series of programs called *This Is War* were suggested by the White House and created by networks. They were broadcast simultaneously by all four networks for thirty minutes each week for thirteen weeks. The shows were highly praised and heard by about 20 million listeners.

The government also used radio to broadcast the basic messages of home-front life: Buy war bonds, save kitchen fats, work hard at your job, and remember the soldiers fighting overseas.

Roosevelt's Fireside Chats

During the darkest days of the Great Depression, President Franklin Roosevelt began delivering popular Sunday night radio broadcasts called "fireside chats." The term *fireside chat* was inspired by Roosevelt's press secretary, who said the president liked to think of his audience as a few people around a fire. The public, in turn, pictured the president relaxing in front of the White House fireplace. Roosevelt's easy speaking style made citizens feel that the president was personally addressing them—not 70 million people as was the reality.

Roosevelt carefully rehearsed each speech. He used simple words, concrete examples, and everyday analogies to make his points. He looked for words that would be used during informal conversations between friends. The president also maintained a relaxed, reassuring manner even when talking about the bleakest of topics.

The first chats in the spring and summer of 1933 focused on crisis situations caused by the depression. Every year after that Roosevelt delivered two fireside chats. Although the chats tapered off during World War II, Roosevelt broadcasted one after the attack on Pearl Harbor. He gave another speech during the dismal days of February 1942, when the war was going badly for the Allies. Several other war-era fireside chats discussed spies, rubber shortages, and war production. Historians have credited Roosevelt's fireside chats with uniting Americans for the war effort and boosting morale throughout the Great Depression and World War II.

Franklin Roosevelt delivers one of his fireside chats. Roosevelt was the first president to use radio to communicate with the American people.

Hollywood Goes to War

The watchword of the war era was *unity*, and to further that cause the government turned to Hollywood studios. Movies were the era's most popular medium, and Hollywood executives were eager to make movies that promoted patriotism and propaganda. These movies also made record profits as audiences, flush with good-paying war jobs, crowded into the theaters. Unlike some industries that were virtually commandeered by the government, movie studios enjoyed complete freedom—as long as they did not focus on sensitive political issues like racial discrimination and food shortages.

Initially Hollywood was afraid the government would go into the business of making movies, a powerful medium of persuasion and manipulation, but it was a groundless fear. To make sure the government would not become involved, movie producers turned out dozens of patriotic movies during the war.

Some of those movies included *Sergeant York* (1941), which features an Oscar-winning performance by Gary Cooper, who plays a young rural sharpshooter who becomes a celebrated World War I hero when he attacks a German position using the same strategy as in a turkey shoot. In *Flying Tigers* (1942), John Wayne commands a unit of the famed Flying Tigers fighter pilots who fought the Japanese in China before America's entry into World War II. *So Proudly We Hail!* (1943) was a love story about women at the fighting front who recall their experiences in combat and in love. *Since You Went Away* (1944) is a sentimental portrait of the World War II home front with its trials,

Gary Cooper played a World War I hero in the film Sergeant York. *War movies were one of the most popular forms of entertainment.*

fears, heartbreaks, and its tribute to family values.

Other well-known war movies of that era include *Yanks in the R.A.F., Dive Bomber, The Fleet's In, Star-Spangled Rhythm, God Is My Co-Pilot,* and *Keep Your Powder Dry.* Top stars of the day were Clark Gable, Bob Hope, Spencer Tracy, Gary Cooper, Betty Grable, Bette Davis, Judy Garland, Humphrey Bogart, and Bing Crosby.

Movie actors and producers were considered so important to the war effort that major stars, directors, and writers were allowed draft deferments. Although they were allowed to remain safe at home, they were virtually drafted as war workers and volunteers. Besides starring in prowar movies, many stars doubled as air raid spotters and wardens. In addition, their talents were put to use at home and overseas to entertain troops in person.

Hollywood films glorified the prototypical American hero. A humble American soldier could always beat fifty Japanese single-handedly. The FBI always caught sneaky saboteurs and broke up spy rings. The heroes never died and always returned home to their sweethearts. On the other hand, the Nazis were always portrayed as cultured but brutally evil. These roles were sometimes played by German actors who lived in the United States. The Japanese were shown as fanatical, sneaky, and dirty fighters. The roles of these villains were played by Chinese Americans, Korean Americans, or even Caucasian actors wearing makeup. Peter Lorre was so adept at playing evil characters that he played both Nazi and Japanese villains.

At the beginning of the war, many films lacked realism and were simply efforts to promote patriotism and unity. Later, after the United States began to win the war, films took a more realistic turn, based on actual events. The most authentic war films were released at the end of the war. *Thirty Seconds over Tokyo* (1944) is a detailed true story of the "Doolittle Raid," in which Colonel Jimmy Doolittle, played by Van Johnson, is stung by the attack on Pearl Harbor and devises a plan for a daring raid on the heart of Japan itself. *The Story of G.I. Joe* portrayed the true horrors faced by American soldiers.

War films were popular because there was a great public need for information about the war, even if it was re-created and artificial in form.

War Songs

Popular wartime music was intensely patriotic. The top composers of the day answered the war's call with popular songs meant to inspire men to great battlefield deeds. Loneliness, love, and separation were always popular song themes, but during the war these themes took on special meaning. It was not unusual for a battle-hardened soldier in the Pacific to shed a tear when hearing Bing Crosby softly croon the popular "White Christmas."

The Hollywood Canteen

The idea of the Hollywood Canteen was conceived by actors Bette Davis and John Garfield (who was classified 4-F by the army). To start the project, Davis rallied to raise money for the Hollywood Canteen Foundation. With the help of carpenters, technicians, and forty-two unions that worked for movie studios—and who donated their services—the Hollywood Canteen became a reality. The Hollywood Canteen opened on October 17, 1942, in what was once an old barn at 1451 Cahuenga Boulevard. The canteen welcomed all men and women in uniform. It also attracted some of Hollywood's most glamorous stars, who washed dishes, served crullers and coffee, and danced the foxtrot and jitterbug with military personnel.

In a 1943 interview with *Colliers* magazine, Bette Davis had this to say about the Hollywood Canteen. It was reprinted in Robert Heide and John Gilman's *Home Front America.*

> The Hollywood Canteen was created with one idea in mind—to give men in the armed forces some fun and a chance to meet personally the people of the entertainment world of Hollywood. We can always tell when a boy has seen actual battle. They have something in their eyes. There was a marine here last night who said to me, "You'll never know what it means to see girls and hear music. Just let me sit please."

Servicemen and women at the canteen might find themselves drinking coffee and chatting with Rita Hayworth, Barbara Stanwyck, Dorothy Lamour, Claudette Colbert, or Bette Davis herself.

About 2,500 soldiers visited the Hollywood Canteen every night; it is estimated that over 3 million were served in the canteen during the war.

American military personnel are entertained at the Hollywood Canteen. Popular movie stars volunteered their time and talent here.

Many wartime songs were jingoistic (belligerently nationalistic) or downright silly. Songs had such catchy titles as "The Japs Don't Have a Chinaman's Chance" and "We're Gonna Find a Feller Who Is Yeller and Beat Him Red, White, and Blue." Some novelty songs had foolish verses such as "Send up in smokio / the city of Tokyo / Show the Nipponese / that Uncle Sam does not jokio!"[44]

Songs of the Great Depression had focused on pennies falling from heaven, bluebirds flying over the rainbow, and other happy themes. Popular songs of World War II dwelled on sadder themes. Moody songs such as "I'll Walk Alone," "Sentimental Journey," and "I'll Never Smile Again," spoke of loss and loneliness.

Swing Music and Glenn Miller

The most popular musical style during the war was swing music played by big bands. These ten- to twenty-piece bands were divided into instrumental sections. The rhythm section—piano, guitar, bass, and drums—maintained a steady, even beat. Meanwhile, saxophone and brass sections countered each other with harmonized riffs while soloists improvised over this background.

Popular big bands were led by conductors, writers, and arrangers such as Benny Goodman, Fletcher Henderson, Duke Ellington, and brothers Tommy and Jimmy Dorsey. The Glenn Miller Orchestra was the most popular big band—and one that best represented the sound of the time.

Every Tuesday, Wednesday, and Thursday at 7:15 P.M., Americans could tune in their radios to hear the sounds of the Glenn Miller Orchestra. Miller sold hundreds of thousands of records playing his hits such as "Chattanooga Choo Choo," "Moonlight Serenade," "Tuxedo Junction," "The Booglie Wooglie Piggy," and "I've Got a Gal in Kalamazoo."

In 1942 Miller attempted to enlist his entire band into the navy's entertainment unit but was turned down. Miller then offered his services to the army. The army said yes to the idea of forming a musical unit to entertain the troops. Besides raising millions of dollars at war-bonds rallies, Miller's big band boosted morale performing for American and Allied soldiers at hundreds of theaters, concert halls, and military bases in Great Britain. He also prerecorded dozens of concerts for airplay on European radio stations. Meanwhile, the bandleader rose in rank from captain to major.

Glenn Miller and his orchestra joined the army and entertained American and Allied troops in Great Britain. Miller died while planning a tour in liberated Paris.

By December 1944—with the Germans driven out of France—Miller boarded a small plane to set up a "victory orchestra" tour in Paris. The plane never arrived at its destination. The air force concluded that Miller's plane went down somewhere over the English Channel. No trace of the aircraft was ever found, and the mystery surrounding his death added to his legend.

The USO

While some lucky soldiers were entertained by big bands, most found respite from their troubles at the United Service Organization for National Defense (USO). The USO was established by the government in February 1941 with a $15-million grant. That amount was quickly matched by private and public contributions. Initially five civilian organizations formed the USO: the YMCA, YWCA, Salvation Army, National Catholic Community Services, and the National Jewish Welfare Board. These groups brought in service organizations such as the Elks, the Moose Club, and the American Legion.

USOs near military camps and in big cities created a home away from home for America's 12 million military personnel. USO drop-ins were hosted by young women and housewives who served coffee, milk, and donuts. Soldiers simply rested, played cards, or read books and magazines. The USO Victory Campaign (in association with the American Library Association) collected 13 million books and 3 million magazines for this purpose.

Frank Sinatra

Singer Frank Sinatra was one of the biggest musical sensations of the World War II era and the first to cause mass hysteria among teenage girls (called "bobby-soxers"). The skinny young man from Hoboken, New Jersey, was 4-F because of a punctured eardrum, but Sinatra's smooth voice caused teenage girls to swoon. He also made the word *crooner* a household word.

In 1944 thirty thousand bobby-soxers surrounded Manhattan's Paramount Theater, where Sinatra was giving a concert. Seven hundred policemen had to be called in to quell the near riot that resulted. Sinatra was blamed for teenage truancy and was even denounced in Congress as one of the prime instigators of delinquency in American juveniles.

Sinatra went on to impress older crowds as he broke attendance records at New York's Waldorf-Astoria. Before long, the crooner was a national star and a regular in many Hollywood movies.

Frank Sinatra (right of center) makes his way through a crowd of adoring bobby-soxers.

In addition to the service clubs, the USO operated a haven for rest and recreation at the Royal Hawaiian Hotel, where battle-fatigued submariners and aviators returning from dangerous missions in the

Pacific could unwind. The USO also organized 228 national touring companies overseas to play the "Foxhole Circuit" on hundreds of army bases.

Between 1941 and 1947 the USO produced over four hundred thousand performances, which were seen by 200 million people. Many shows were led by Bob Hope and featured comedy, singing, and dancing. These performances included the biggest stars of the day, including Bing Crosby, Laurel and Hardy, Jack Benny, Ingrid Bergman, Dinah Shore, Marlene Dietrich, the Andrews Sisters, and others. Some performers spent up to eight months and traveled thirty-seven thousand miles playing a single tour for men and women in the military.

Bob Hope amuses the troops during a USO tour. The USO went overseas with Hollywood's most popular movie stars, singers, and musicians.

Like every other American industry, the media and entertainment industries pitched in to do their part for the war effort. Some reporters and entertainers even died in the line of duty. The hard work and dedication of the people in these businesses did so much to raise the morale of soldiers and citizens that their contribution to the war was considered as important as any other.

The End of the War and Beyond

Franklin Roosevelt was reelected to an unprecedented fourth term in 1944. America was an entirely different place than when Roosevelt first came to office in 1932. The economic problems faced by average Americans were stunningly solved by the war. Unemployment went from 25 percent to nearly zero, farm prices were up, and business growth was phenomenal.

On April 12, 1945, sixty-three-year-old President Roosevelt died of a cerebral hemorrhage. After more than twelve years in office, Roosevelt was such a familiar figure to most Americans that his passing had the same impact as a death in the family. When Americans heard the news, many stopped what they were doing and wept. A special train bore the president's body north from Washington, D.C., to his home in New York. As the train took the president to his final resting place, tens of thousands of Americans gathered next to the train tracks to say good-bye. Vice President Harry S Truman was sworn in as president.

Harry S Truman became president after Franklin Roosevelt died suddenly on April 12, 1945, one month before Germany surrendered to the Allies.

Roosevelt did not live to see the Germans surrender unconditionally to the Allies on May 7, 1945, after almost six years at war. The day after that, surrender was proclaimed V-E (Victory in Europe) Day—coincidentally it was Truman's birthday. Millions of people crowded into the streets of American cities to celebrate with ticker-tape parades, cheering, drinking, and dancing.

On August 6, 1945, the United States dropped an atomic bomb on Hiroshima, Japan, headquarters of the Japanese regional army and a manufacturing center for military equipment. Almost five square miles of the city were destroyed by the first atomic blast to ever be used in wartime. More than seventy thousand people were killed immediately, and thousands died afterward as a result of radiation poisoning.

The terrible devastation wreaked by the second atomic bomb can be seen in this photo of Nagasaki.

On August 9 a second atomic bomb was dropped on Nagasaki, a shipbuilding center. The second blast killed thirty-six thousand people and wounded more than forty thousand. Japan surrendered to the Allies on August 14, 1945. This day was known as V-J (Victory in Japan) Day. World War II was officially over on September 2, when Japanese emperor Hirohito signed surrender agreements aboard the battleship USS *Missouri*.

The Face of a Changed Country

By any standard or measure, the United States was a different country at the end of World War II. The war began with the country mired in a depression. When it ended, America was the richest and strongest country in the world.

The gross national product—the measure of the nation's total production of goods and services—had jumped from $90 billion in 1939 to $213 billion in 1944. The federal budget soared from $9 billion in 1939 to $98.4 billion. Federal outlays for scientific research increased from $74 million in 1940 to $1.6 billion in 1945.

During the war the federal government had instilled itself into nearly every aspect of American life. The government functioned more or less as a partner with industry, labor, farming, medicine, education, and science. And in doing so, the size of the government swelled from 1 million employees in 1939 to 3.8 million in 1945—an increase of 380 percent.

After the government, the biggest growth occurred in farming. Total farm income in 1945 reached $24 billion—an increase of 250 percent over 1939.

Another wartime growth spurt occurred in America's colleges and universities. The Army Specialized Training Program had 140,000 soldiers enrolled in colleges by 1943. The Navy College Training Program had 80,000. Within a few years of the war's end, over 1.5 million servicemen and women had enrolled in college at the government's expense.

Wartime Inventions

At the outbreak of World War II, Germany was one of the most technologically advanced countries in the world. Its scientists led the way in chemistry, weapons development, and rocket science. The need to beat the Germans imposed such heavy demands on America's scientific community that, in 1941, Roosevelt created the Office of Scientific Research and Development (OSRD) to coordinate scientific development. The OSRD commanded the services of thirty thousand physicians, chemists, lawyers, business managers, generals, admirals, laborers, and civil servants. One of the greatest achievements of the OSRD was the development of penicillin. The lifesaving antibiotic was first used to prevent blood poisoning and infection in wounded soldiers.

Other inventions that came out of the war not only changed the outcome of the

One of the many discoveries that came out of World War II was penicillin (pictured). The drug saved millions of lives during and after the war.

fighting but also changed life for Americans when the fighting ended. Military innovations such as improved telecommunications, aerodynamics, and radar all had peacetime uses.

The advancement of computer science also received a boost by the war. Computers were first pioneered at the Massachusetts Institute of Technology (MIT) in the 1930s and improved dramatically during the war. But they were nothing like today's computers. In 1942 the gigantic computer at MIT weighed 100 tons, had 2,000 vacuum tubes, 150 electric motors, and 200 miles of wire.

Other wartime production breakthroughs allowed mass production of air conditioning and television once the war was over. Likewise, new plastics and other synthetic materials found uses in thousands of products.

Peacetime production of consumer goods resumed with the same drive and intensity that had been used to win the war. Factories that had been making hand grenades, machine guns, and bombs returned to making consumer goods that were in short supply. According to reporter Jack Altshul, who was quoted in *America Remembers the Home Front,*

> The war was the dividing line between depression and the prosperity that followed. And what it took to get that was the boys that were killed. It was a stiff price to pay. Up to that time, twenty dollars a week was a manageable salary. Many people would have signed away their souls for a hundred-dollars-a-week job for life. . . . Then all of a sudden you get the wartime boom, and just as suddenly a few years later the war is over. Luxuries that only millionaires could have, before the war, suddenly became available to everybody on credit—refrigerators, televisions, dishwashers, washing machines.[45]

The severe housing shortage caused by the war fueled a building boom across America. Cornfields, farmhouses, and apple orchards fell to thousands of suburban housing tracts and strip malls. By the end of the 1950s, these new neighborhoods would be connected by forty-one thousand miles of brand new freeways.

Levitton, New York, the first housing development in America. Such tracts would spring up all over the United States after the war.

These too were constructed with nearly the speed and determination that had been used to fight the Nazis.

All this comfort and prosperity, and the relief that the war had ended, fueled a baby boom unprecedented in American history. Between 1946 and 1964, 30 million children were born—more than 4 million a year after the mid-1950s. This "baby boom" formed a huge population bubble that influenced everything from the sale of diapers and cars to the growing popularity of rock-and-roll music— and still does today.

The Continuing Effect of the War

Life on the home front during World War II was difficult, exciting, joyous, and sorrowful. Many of those who lived through the time look back fondly at a simpler time when millions of Americans could act as one, putting their total faith and trust in the government to do what was right. But home-front nostalgia must never shadow the true cost of the war. Over 400,000 young Americans were killed in World War II, and another 670,000 GIs were wounded. Across the globe more than 45 million people died in World War II. War-related famines in India and China killed another 15 million.

Most of those killed in Europe and Asia were civilians. Few American civilians became casualties; a few hundred nonmilitary personnel were killed at Pearl Harbor, and six others died in Oregon from a Japanese balloon bomb. Other civilians came in harm's way overseas and were killed, wounded, or taken prisoner. In all, civilian casualties totaled several thousand.

World War II was not a final event but the beginning of an ongoing process. With Germany, France, and Great Britain greatly weakened by the war, the Soviet Union became the strongest country in Europe. The smoke had barely cleared from the battlefields before the Soviets

The end of World War II did not mean the end of fear. Many Americans built home bomb shelters (pictured) to protect themselves in case of nuclear war.

and the United States became locked in a power struggle that would lead to a massive nuclear buildup on both sides and a bitter struggle known as the Cold War. The fear of the Soviets marching across Europe as the Nazis had once done, struck fear into the hearts of millions. This caused the defense buildup begun in 1940 to continue unabated until the end of the Cold War in 1990. Information about the construction of nuclear weapons has spread from top-secret government installations in the 1940s to dozens of other nations across the globe.

At the beginning of the twenty-first century, the World War II generation is passing into history. But it is vitally necessary to remember the dedication, determination, and unshakable convictions that generation demonstrated in so many aspects of their lives. Mistakes were made—especially against Japanese Americans and other minorities, but the World War II–era Americans genuinely did beat a great evil and save the world for democracy. Some paid the ultimate price for that freedom. Many more suffered through tough times. But most rose above and beyond the call of duty to make America the strong, prosperous, and free nation that it is today.

★ Notes ★

Introduction: Before the War

1. Quoted in Associated Press, *Twentieth-Century America: A Primary Source Collection from the Associated Press: World War II, 1939–1945*. New York: Grolier, 1995, p. 68.

Chapter 1: Preparing for War

2. Quoted in Associated Press, *Twentieth-Century America*, p. 76.
3. Quoted in Associated Press, *Twentieth-Century America*, p. 76.
4. Quoted in Ronald H. Bailey, *The Home Front, U.S.A.* Alexandria, VA: Time-Life Books, 1977, p. 8.
5. Quoted in Ezra Bowen, ed., *This Fabulous Century: 1940–1950.* New York: Time-Life, 1969, p. 170.
6. Quoted in Bailey, *The Home Front, U.S.A.*, p. 47.
7. Quoted in Bailey, *The Home Front, U.S.A.*, p. 47.
8. Lee Kennett, *G.I.: The American Soldier in World War II.* New York: Scribner, 1987, p. 55.

Chapter 2: Bringing the War Home

9. Quoted in Bailey, *The Home Front, U.S.A.*, p. 26.
10. Quoted in Nate Polowetzky, ed., *World War II.* New York: Henry Holt, 1989, p. 87.
11. Quoted in Richard R. Lingeman, *Don't You Know There's a War On?* New York: G. P. Putnam's Sons, 1970, p. 56.
12. Quoted in Bailey, *The Home Front, U.S.A.*, p. 105.
13. Quoted in Polowetzky, ed., *World War II*, p. 147.
14. Quoted in Roy Hoopes, *America Remembers the Home Front.* New York: Hawthorn Books, 1977, p. 310.
15. Quoted in Hoopes, *America Remembers the Home Front*, p. 310.

Chapter 3: Family Life During the War

16. Quoted in Robert Heide and John Gilman, *Home Front America: Popular Culture of the World War II Era.* San Francisco: Chronicle Books, 1995, p. 55.
17. Quoted in Heide and Gilman, *Home Front America*, p. 68.
18. Quoted in Heide and Gilman, *Home Front America*, p. 58.
19. Quoted in Heide and Gilman, *Home Front America*, p. 61.
20. Quoted in Heide and Gilman, *Home Front America*, p. 57.

Chapter 4: The Arsenal of Democracy

21. Quoted in Don Larson, *An Album of World War II Home Fronts.* New York: Franklin Watts, 1980, p. 64.
22. Quoted in Bailey, *The Home Front, U.S.A.,* p. 77.
23. Quoted in Cabell Phillips, *The 1940s.* New York: Macmillan, 1975, p. 104.
24. Quoted in Polowetzky, *World War II,* p. 99.
25. Quoted in Bowen, *This Fabulous Century,* p. 148.
26. Quoted in Frank Freidel, *Franklin D. Roosevelt: A Rendezvous with Destiny.* Boston: Little, Brown, 1990, p. 348.
27. Quoted in Bailey, *The Home Front, U.S.A.,* p. 143.
28. Quoted in Bailey, *The Home Front, U.S.A.,* p. 90.
29. Quoted in Kenneth Paul O'Brien and Lynn Hudson, eds., *The Home-Front War: World War II and American Society.* Westport, CT: Greenwood Press, 1995, p. 99.

Chapter 5: Racial Hostility Against Americans

30. Quoted in Bailey, *The Home Front, U.S.A.,* p. 26.
31. Quoted in Archie Satterfield, *The Home Front.* New York: Playboy Press, 1981, p. 305.
32. Quoted in Bailey, *The Home Front, U.S.A.,* p. 39.
33. *Quoted in Bailey, The Home Front, U.S.A.,* p. 55.
34. Quoted in Polowetzky, *World War II,* p. 151.
35. Quoted in Polowetzky, *World War II,* p. 151.
36. Quoted in Fred Stanton, ed., *Fighting Racism in World War II.* New York: Pathfinder, 1980, p. 312.
37. Quoted in Bailey, *The Home Front, U.S.A.,* p. 149.
38. Quoted in O'Brien and Hudson, *The Home-Front War,* p. 19.

Chapter 6: News and Entertainment

39. Quoted in John Morton Blum, *V Was for Victory: Politics and American Culture During World War II.* New York: Harcourt Brace Jovanovich, 1976, p. 31.
40. Quoted in Blum, *V Was for Victory,* p. 22.
41. Quoted in Lingeman, *Don't You Know There's a War On?,* p. 303.
42. Quoted in Hoopes, *America Remembers the Home Front,* p. 375.
43. Quoted in Bailey, *The Home Front, U.S.A.,* p. 115.
44. Quoted in William M. Tuttle, *"Daddy's Gone to War."* New York: Oxford University Press, 1993, p. 152.

Epilogue: The End of the War and Beyond

45. Quoted in Hoopes, *America Remembers the Home Front,* p. 371.

★ For Further Reading ★

Ronald H. Bailey, *The Home Front, U.S.A.* Alexandria, VA: Time-Life Books, 1977. Another of the great books published by Time-Life, this volume is full of award-winning photographs, fascinating facts, and history about the home front.

Stan B. Cohen, *V for Victory: America's Home Front During World War II.* Missoula, MT: Pictorial Histories, 1991. A pictorial history of the home front with four hundred pages of photographs, reprinted newspaper articles, World War II–era posters, magazine covers, food labels, and other memorabilia.

Penny Colman, *Rosie the Riveter: Women Working on the Home Front in World War II.* New York: Crown, 1995. A book for young adults with in-depth coverage of home-front women's contributions to the war effort. Great photographs of women building airplanes, welding, servicing locomotives, and building bombs.

Robert Heide and John Gilman, *Home Front America: Popular Culture of the World War II Era.* San Francisco: Chronicle Books, 1995. A nostalgic and visual look at the paraphernalia and kitschy culture of the home-front era. Written with humor and warmth.

Roy Hoopes, *America Remembers the Home Front.* New York: Hawthorn Books, 1977. A book composed entirely of source quotes from people who lived through home-front experiences ranging from witnessing the attack at Pearl Harbor to supervising air-raid drills and working in defense plants.

Lee Kennett, *G.I.: The American Soldier in World War II.* New York: Scribner, 1987. The detailed story of the GIs' life in the U.S. armed forces during World War II covers topics concerning the draft, basic training, the challenges of combat, and the dead and wounded.

Richard R. Lingeman, *Don't You Know There's a War On?* New York: G. P. Putnam's Sons, 1970. Written by a former writer for the *New York Times Book Review,* this book covers all aspects of home-front America in a witty and educational style.

Judy Barrett Litoff and David C. Smith, *Since You Went Away: World War II Letters from American Women on the Home Front.* New York: Oxford University Press, 1991. A book of letters by average women during the war to husbands, fathers, brothers, and boyfriends. These letters capture intimate details of each woman's life and the greater transformations that were taking place in society at large.

★ Works Consulted ★

Associated Press, *Twentieth Century America: A Primary Source Collection from the Associated Press: World War II 1939–1945*. New York: Grolier, 1995. A book composed entirely of articles written by Associated Press reporters during World War II. Besides covering the war from Fascist expansion in Europe to V-J Day, the book has a large section on the home front.

Ezra Bowen, ed., *This Fabulous Century: 1940–1950*. New York: Time-Life, 1969. An oversized book with hundreds of pictures. The photos and text cover the entire war, from the silly to the deadly serious, and include battle photos as well as pictures of rationing, movie stars, and the war's aftermath.

John Morton Blum, *V Was for Victory: Politics and American Culture During World War II*. New York: Harcourt Brace Jovanovich, 1976. A scholarly work from a professor of history at Yale University that focuses on the politics and prejudices of the era.

Frank Freidel, *Franklin D. Roosevelt: A Rendezvous with Destiny*. Boston: Little, Brown, 1990. A book that details the life of America's longest-serving president, Franklin Delano Roosevelt, who oversaw America's mobilization and major battles in World War II.

Doris Kearns Goodwin, *No Ordinary Time*. New York: Simon & Schuster, 1994. A complete chronicle of the Roosevelt presidency and the complex relationship between Franklin and Eleanor Roosevelt during a time of national crisis.

Susan M. Hartmann, *The Home Front and Beyond: American Women in the 1940s*. Boston: Twayne, 1982. A book written by a history professor at the University of Missouri that discusses women's place in the war, including the work environment, women in the service, women in politics, and women's education.

Don Larson, *An Album of World War II Home Fronts*. New York: Franklin Watts, 1980. An easy-to-read book that covers the home fronts of several countries involved in World War II. Besides discussing life on the American home front, the book shows what life was like on the Japanese home front, the German home front, and others.

Kenneth Paul O'Brien and Lynn Hudson, eds., *The Home-Front War: World War II and American Society*. Westport, CT: Greenwood Press, 1995. A recent book, each chapter is written by an expert who analyzes the political and social layers of the home front ranging from how the Constitution was subverted by Japanese internment to propaganda in the media.

Cabell Phillips, *The 1940s*. New York: Macmillan, 1975. A detailed book by a prominent member of the *New York Times'* Washington staff. The book contains more than seventy photographs and gives an illuminating history of the decade, discussing the men, women, and institutions that came together to fight the world war.

Nate Polowetzky, ed., *World War II*. New York: Henry Holt, 1989. A book that covers World War II from Pearl Harbor to the dropping of the atom bomb as described and seen by the writers and photographers of the Associated Press news organization.

Archie Satterfield, *The Home Front*. New York: Playboy Press, 1981. A book about the American home front with extended quotes from people who were involved. Chapters feature eye-witness accounts of Pearl Harbor, women in defense plants, men joining the military, victims of prejudice, wartime entertainment, and other subjects.

Fred Stanton, ed., *Fighting Racism in World War II*. New York: Pathfinder, 1980. The story of the struggles of black racism, Jim Crow laws, black workers in industry, and other African-American struggles during World War II. Stories are taken from the pages of the socialist newsweekly *Militant*, which was published during the 1940s.

William M. Tuttle, *"Daddy's Gone to War."* New York: Oxford University Press, 1993. A book that analyzes the psychological effects of World War II on children. Topics include fears and nightmares after Pearl Harbor, working mothers, children playing war games, and dealing with the death of a loved one.

☆ Index ☆

★ Picture Credits ★

Cover photo: Digital Stock
American Stock/Archive Photos, 62
Anthony Potter Collection/Archive Photos, 78
APA/Archive Photos, 18
Archive Photos, 42, 44, 45, 47, 58, 77, 79, 92, 93
Corbis, 12, 24, 32, 61, 74, 82
Corbis-Bettmann, 16, 25, 28, 29, 38, 40, 48, 53 (bottom), 57, 88, 91, 94 (top), 99
Corbis/Hulton-Deutsch, 41
Corbis/Lake County Museum, 26
Corbis/Seattle Post-Intelligencer Collection; Museum of History and Industry, 34
Digital Stock, 7
FPG International, 15, 17, 20, 21, 22, 31 (left), 51, 54, 81, 85, 90, 98
Lambert/Archive Photos, 43
Library of Congress, 9 (bottom), 11, 14, 63 (bottom), 94 (bottom)
Lineworks, Incorporated, 30
Los Alamos National Laboratory, 63 (top)
National Archives, 9 (top), 10, 13, 27, 31 (right), 35, 37, 49, 50, 53 (top), 56, 67, 69 (top), 70, 71, 73, 75, 86, 87, 95
National Japanese American Historical Society, 69 (bottom)
The National Portrait Gallery/Smithsonian Institution, 83
Popperfoto/Archive Photos, 97
Smithsonian Institution, 60

★ About the Author ★

Stuart A. Kallen is the author of more than 135 nonfiction books for children and young adults. He has written on topics ranging from the theory of relativity to rock-and-roll history and life on the American frontier. Mr. Kallen lives in San Diego, California.